AF251427

WHAT'S YOUR EXCUSE?

WHAT'S YOUR EXCUSE?

Barbara Arnstein

CASTLE

Copyright © 1990 Castle Books
a division of Book Sales, Inc.
110 Enterprise Avenue
Secaucus, NJ 07094

All rights reserved.
No part of this book may be reproduced or transmitted in any form or by any means, electronic or mechanical, including photocopying, recording, or by any information storage and retrieval system, without permission in writing from the Publisher.

Manufactured in the United States of America.
ISBN: 1-55521-546-5

Contents

Introduction

It's time to retire those flimsy, threadbare excuses you've been using and learn all new ones! To start you off, a few excuses for reading this book:

1. Making excuses is a time-honored tradition. Everyone throughout history has made them at one time or another, beginning with Eve who said, "The snake made me do it."
2. Used properly, excuses can smooth out your troubled relationships, endear you to authority figures and provide you with more leisure time.
3. If you are a terrible liar, you will be a better one after reading this book.

This book includes excuses to use on your husband, your wife, your parents, your boss, your in-laws, your friends and many more of the people you know. But don't make any excuses now–start reading right away!

Good Reasons for Being Late to Work

I had to take the bus because I'm not on the best speaking terms with my talking car. It's literally been driving me up a wall!

I accidentally played my exercise videotape in slow motion, so it took me and Jane Fonda forever to finish our morning exercises.

My new alarm clock is defective. It only goes off when I'm asleep.

I stopped at the barber shop this morning and the barber took an unusually long time with my hair. I told him, "Ten years ago it didn't take you this long to make my hair look this full," and do you know what HIS excuse was? "I'm sorry. I was 10 years younger then."

I heard on the morning news that the air today is rated "unacceptable" and I spent a long time wondering how to commute without breathing.

This morning I waited for hours for the light to change–until I realized I was in a red-light district.

On the radio this morning I listened to the Emergency Broadcast Test and I tried to pull myself together. I get so unnerved when I hear that thing that I think they ought to call it the Public Nervous Announcement.

If you're an hour late, you might try this drastic solution: hobble into work on crutches, with casts on both arms and a bandage around your head. Then say, "I'm sorry I'm late, but this morning I fell from a sixth-story window." Your boss should buy this explanation. He may even give you a bonus for your unusual dedication. Come to think of it, I doubt he'll respond the way one boss did to this excuse. His reaction was, "And that took you an hour?"

I went to pick up some cigarettes and somebody stepped on my hand.

Why go with that moldy oldy, "I forgot to set my clock back for daylight-saving time" when you can use this nifty new excuse: "I thought daylight SPENDING time just started, so I spent another hour in bed."

Don't use a common excuse such as, "I'm late because I thought I spotted Elvis at the A&P–and I checked every aisle to make sure I hadn't." Use a similar one with an original twist, for example: "I saw Elvis at the A&P this morning–and he was buying so much junk food that I didn't get through the check-out line until just now."

I overslept because I moonlight as a manicurist and, last night, a special customer took HOURS–Freddy Kruger came in to have his steel tips filed!

When you excuse yourself for being late, be sure that the blame is put right where it belongs–on anyone but you! Don't be like the man who arrived late to work one morning with bandages on both of his ears. When his boss asked him what happened he said, "Well, it was like this. I was ironing when the phone range–and without thinking, I put the iron to my ear." His boss then asked, "What happened to the other one?" and he replied, "The idiot called back."

The boss never heard this one: "On the way to work this morning I passed one of those old-fashioned, giant building clocks. The big hand had about 10 feet to go before it reached 9 a.m., so I figured I had all the time in the world!"

Around the Christmas season you can try this one: "My true love actually sent me a partridge in a pear tree. The stupid bird made a mess of my living room and I spent hours raking off the furniture."

If your boss is interested in running, how about trying this one? "Last Friday my doctor told me to start running 5 miles every morning. I just talked to his and found out that I misunderstood his instructions–so I'll be in to work as soon as I can travel 15 miles."

Although I was promised delivery before 9 a.m., I'm still waiting for my:

a. new sofa
b. Fudgie the Whale ice-cream cake
c. Biggest Hits of Peter Lemongello album
d. Slim Whitman record set
e. tax refund from 1962
f. Captain Midnight decoder ring (I was told I could expect it any day now.)

How to Be a Hero to Kids

After children have been told about Santa Claus, they frequently become disillusioned when they see him in every department store an on every street corner, ringing Salvation Army bells. When you child asks you if there really is a Santa Claus, you can protect his blissful innocence by answering, "Of course there is. Who do you think these people are dressed as?"

If you've told your child that prayer can accomplish anything, the odds are that he's prayed for some toy or game that never materialized. If he approaches you with that tough question, "Why didn't God listen to me?" just give him this perfect excuse: "He did listen to you–he just said no."

Children love status symbols as much as adults do, and if you've agreed to get your child a dog, chances are he begged you to get a pedigreed pooch. Get him a mutt, and explain that it's a police dog working undercover. He'll be thrilled!

The Whole Truth

Making excuses doesn't necessarily have to involve lying. If you're the type who has a conscience, you should try these lines:

STATEMENT OF FACT	TRANSLATION
No salesman will call.	He'll just go directly to your home.
Money refunded if not satisfactory.	If we find your money to be satisfactory, we'll keep it.
This won't hurt a bit.	It won't hurt ME a bit, but YOU will feel excruciating agony.
Bill Cosby doesn't have the talent you do.	You have no real talent.
These pictures don't do you justice.	These pictures make you look attractive.
You've never looked more beautiful.	There is no hope for your looks.
You look like a model.	You look like a smaller imitation of the real thing.
I've never seen a baby look like yours.	I've never seen a baby uglier than yours.

If you run a diner, you can put a sign in the window that says, "Mom's Home Cooking."

If anyone complains about the "homemade" food, tell them it's the plain truth– "Mom is home cooking."

Party Excuses

Entertaining guests and mingling at parties can be fraught with terror and hazards, but the following anecdotes will help.

A famous hostess once went all out for a holiday party to impress her in-laws. She bought a huge turkey with all the trimmings and even hired a serving maid. When the big moment came for the maid to bring out the turkey she tripped, and the bird thudded to the floor. Before her horrified guests could react, the quick-thinking hostess excused the accident with, "No problem. Just bring out their OTHER turkey." With that, she brought the fallen bird back to the kitchen, washed it off, and had the maid serve it again!

An executive at an office Christmas party had too much to drink and blurted to a new female acquaintance, "See that man over there? I hate his guts." She retorted, "Oh, really? That man is my husband." Without missing a beat, he excused his gaffe with, "I know that. That's WHY I hate his guts."

A mail room worker who had too much to drink insulted the company president–when they were standing next to each other. The CEO whirled around and said, "Do you know who I am?" "No, I don't," admitted the worker. "I'm the president of this company!" he roared. "Do you know who I am?" the worker asked. "No, I don't." said the president. "Thank goodness!," shouted the worker, as he ran, not through rain, sleet or snow, but a sea-of people!

There's nothing worse than being fresh out of excuses when you're faced with doing something you do NOT want to do. A groom who was petrified of speaking in public was hauled to his feet at his wedding–by his "friends"–and urged to say a few words. His mind went totally black, and he blurted out, "First of all, I want to say that this comes as a total shock to me..."

If you're stuck in the receiving line at a wedding–and there's no way you can get out of it–you might try saying something other than the usual phrases of welcome and see if anyone notices. One man who decided to do this shook a guest's hand while murmuring, "you know, my aunt died recently." The guest replied, "Glad to hear it! You should take the same step yourself soon!"

If you dread being asked to speak at testimonial dinners, you might take a trip from the man who was forced to his feet with this compliment: "This man is so witty that all one has to do is put a dinner in his mouth–and out comes a speech!" He cleverly replied, "That's true enough, but put a speech in most people's ears–and out comes their dinner!"

One woman at a family reunion dinner noticed that her young son was filling up his dessert plate over and over again with pastries. She grabbed him and demanded, "What excuse did you give your aunt for being so greedy?" and he answered, "Each time I tell her they're for you."

Asking for Money

Whenever you see a street beggar asking for money, remember it's far from easy to beseech a strange for funds. For thousands of years, beggars have had to create ingenious excuses to coax cash from passer-bys.

A well-dressed executive once asked a beggar, "Why is a healthy, muscular person such as yourself asking for money?" Replied the beggar, "For the 50 cents you give me, should I cut off my arms?"

Another beggar was indignantly asked, "What are you doing asking me for money on the street?" He retorted, "What do you want me to do? Open an office?"

Two mendicants were brought before a judge for vagrancy. The judge asked the first, "What's your excuse for being a vagrant?" The man replied, "I lost my job, my wife divorced me and then I was evicted. Couldn't you find it in your heart to let me go free?" The judge said, "Thirty days." After he was led out, the judge asked the second beggar the same question. He answered, "Uhhh...errr...you see...ohhh...what happened was..." The judge said, "I can't listen to this all day. Case dismissed." When the first one saw his friend leaving, he said, "How come I"m going to jail and you're going free?" Said his friend, "Because you didn't know how to talk to the judge."

The two vagrants were again hauled into court and a different judge asked them, "What's your excuse for vagrancy? Do you have a place to live?" The first vagrant replied, "I live under the beautiful blue sky, in the sheltering arms of Mother Nature, on the bosom of Mother

Earth." The judge said, "That's a very touching sentiment. Case dismissed." The judge then turned to the other vagrant and asked, "Where do you live?" He replied, "I live next door to him."

A well-to-do businessman was stopped on the street by the beggar that he assisted ever week and offered him, instead of money, this excuse: "Mu business went badly this week." Annoyed, the beggar snapped, "Just because *you* had a bad week, why should *I* have to suffer?"

One beggar, who was considered dimwitted, was continually given the choice of taking a nickel or a dime. Each time he took the nickel because it was bigger, and the giver would roar with laughter. Someone once said to him, "I know you know the difference between a nickel and a dime. So why do you always take the nickel?" "Because," the beggar replied, "if I didn't, people would stop doing it."

One family who took in a poor relation for the holidays was sorry–when he stayed for the next holiday–and the next–and the one after that. Finally, he packed his bags and left, but returned the very next day. When the exasperated family asked why, his excuse was, "I figured that when I left, you would feel like celebrating–so I'm here for the celebration!"

At one dinner a permanent visiting relative enjoyed, the family served hors d'oeuvres, including crackers with dip and caviar. The freeloader loaded up on the caviar, until his host protested, "You know, the caviar is much more expensive." His guest continued to stuff himself with it, while offering the excuse, "It's worth it!"

One man who was out of money sat down at a coffee shop counter and ordered a jelly doughnut. "No, make that a Danish," he said. When the check came, he said, "Please don't charge me for the Danish–I traded a jelly doughnut for it." "Pay for the jelly doughnut," said the waitress. " But I didn't eat the jelly doughnut," was his ready excuse.

Great Excuses in History

These excuses belong in the category of understatement excuses. They are excuses that were made when their creators were tired of questions about their fame, or simply wanted to fend off silly questions.

Theory of Relativity creator Albert Einstein didn't say a word until he was three years old (I'll bet it was because he was busy thinking.) He broke his silence one night during dinner with his family, when he suddenly commented, "The soup is cold." Surprised and delighted, his mother blurted out, "Albert! Whey didn't you speak until now?" and his answer was, "Up till now, everything was fine."

When President Kennedy was asked how he would up becoming a hear in World war II, he said, "It was purely involuntary. They sunk my battleship.

When notorious bank robber Willie Sutton was asked why he spent his time robbing banks, he said, "Because that's where the money is."

When playwright Oscar Wilde was asked why he was so promiscuous, he simply "explained": "I can resist anything but temptation."

Sticky Situations

Good evening and welcome to What's Your Excuse?, the program that puts you on the spot for fun and prizes. Ready for the first round?

Imagine that you're forced to endure an evening at the theater with a date you hate. When you can't stand being there another minute, would you:

a. complain of a headache

b. complain of a stomach ache

c. sneak out at intermission and explain the next day: "I read in the program that the second act took place five hours later, and I didn't want to wait that long."

Suppose a regular customer at your grocery store complains that the (closed) grocery store across the street has a sign advertising honeydew for $2 less than you charge. Would you:

a. blame your overhead

b. mention that they have greater volume

c. explain that when YOUR store is closed, you sell them for that price too.

If you were caught red-handed cramming your face with food right after you announced that you were beginning a strict, new diet, would you:

a. plead starvation

b. say, "It's a sin to waste leftovers."

c. explain, "I'm preparing to pose for a 'Before' photo."

If your boss caught you napping on your desk at work, would you:

a. say you've been working a lot of overtime

b. congratulate him on his choice of office chairs

c. jump to you feet and shout, "I've got it! An idea that will make this company millions!"

Excuses for Kids

If you were left back a grade in school, you might view your problem the way one actor's kid did. He broke the news to his father with, "Dad, congratulate me! I'm being held over for another 10 months!"

If you find yourself in class without the homework you were assigned the night before, you might try this strategy: Ask the teacher, "You wouldn't punish me for something I didn't do, would you?" She will, of course, say "No." When she does, say, "Good. Because I didn't do my homework."

If you just received your report card and found that your history mark is lower than before, try this excuse on a parent: "The marks on my report card will remind you of Benjamin Franklin." When he or she asks, "How is that?" say, "We both went down in history."

One boy's father punished him when he confessed to pushing down a Port-O-San as a Halloween prank. He protested, "But, Dad, you told me that if I told the truth–as Washington did when he cut down his father's cherry tree–you wouldn't punish me!" His father said, "This case is different! When Washington cut down the cherry tree, his father wasn't in it at the time!"

A 8-year-old fell down in the playground but didn't make a sound. When a friend asked him why, he said, "I'm too old to cry, but it hurts too much to laugh."

New Answers to the Same Old Questions

Why aren't you married?

1. I can have anyone I please–but I don't please anyone.
2. I didn't know the last proposal I got would be the last proposal I got.
3. My boyfriend and I are still arguing about ONE WORD. I say a man isn't complete until he marries and he says when a man marries he's finished.

Why are you unemployed?

1. Let me put it this way: Nepotism was never a problem for me until my grandfather got kicked off the board of directors.
2. I'm between engagements. (This is also good for the question above.)
3. I'm not really unemployed. Looking for a full-time job is a full-time job!

How do you keep your marriage going?

1. We hate the children but we stay together for the sake of each other.
2. We want to get a divorce but we're waiting until the children are dead.
3. We go out on the town every week. I stay in the holding pen at police headquarters on Friday, and my wife resided there on Saturday.

Are you religious?

1. I wouldn't mind being born again, but my mother couldn't take the pain.
2. Oh, Lord, not that question again!

3. What was that question again? I was lost in prayer.

Whatever you do, never answer the familiar question in this story the way this girl did...

A businessman was very interested in a beautiful girl and told her that he wanted to marry her. "But you must understand," he said, "that my whole life revolved around business, and I never do business without first getting some free samples." "Free samples??" the girl shouted. "FREE SAMPLES?? I have no intention of giving you any 'free samples!' You won't get them from me!" The businessman was very impressed by her attitude, and was about to propose, when she spoke again. "I won't give you any free samples," she repeated, "but I'll give you references."

Excuses for Teenagers

If you find yourself backstage at a concert with a friend–and you only have one pass between you–remember this: Two teens backstage at a concert were approached by a surly security guard who demanded to see their passes. One took off like a shot, and the guard went right after him. When the guard finally caught him, the teenager, surprisingly, pulled out a perfectly legitimate backstage pass. The guard asked him curiously, "Since you had a pass, why did you run?" The teen answered, "Because my friend didn't."

If you wish your parents would appreciate you more, you might try the following approach.

A teenager who was away at college wracked her brains for a way to excuse failing, and finally wrote:
"Dear Mom and Dad,

I have big news. I'm pregnant, and I'm due any day now. I'm going to quit school and go live with the baby's father. He's an escaped con who's into a variety of drugs.

P.S. I lied about all of the above. All I did was flunk my math midterm. Aren't you relieved?"

It would be that your father is the type who forbade you to wear anything provocative or see-through. One girl defied her father and wore a see-through dress to a disco. She faced her father's angry music when she got home. He roared, "You know I told you never to wear anything see-through!" and her clever excuse was, "No one can see through this dress. I'm in the way."

One 14-year-old's parents gave him a curfew of midnight for dates. He protested, "What difference does it make what time I get back? After all, anything that could happen after midnight could just as well happen before it." His father answered, "That's not exactly true. When I went on dates at your age, it took me until midnight to even *kiss* the girl!"

Excuses for Waiters

Someone I know stopped at a small greasy spoon diner and was shocked to find an old friend there working as a waitress. "Linda!" she gasped, "I never thought you would wind up working in a low-class place like this!" Her friend's haughty reply was, "It's not as bad as you think. I don't EAT here."

If you order a well-done steak and the waiter brings you one that's almost raw, make your complaint clearer than this diner did: After he had been served the barely-cooked steak, he finally caught his waiter's eye, and snapped, "I said, 'WELL DONE'!"–and his waiter blurted out, "Oh, thank you, sir! I don't often get a compliment!"

Here is one answer to the classic question, "What is this fly doing in my soup?": "There's no reason to get upset–how much can a fly drink?"

At one roadside diner, a passing truck driver took one look at the young, pretty waitress and said, "What's your name, sweetie?" She replied, "My name is Eileen, and I know I'm pretty. I live around here, I don't know what's playing at the movie theater and I wouldn't go with you if I did. I live with my brother, who's a professional wrestler, and he almost killed the last truck driver who came in here and wouldn't leave me alone. Now what would you like–a hamburger, a cheeseburger, or some of our homemade apple pie?"

A Grab-Bag of Excuses

A man was waiting impatiently for his wife to finish dressing for a party. Finally he shouted, "Are you ready YET?"and she snapped, "I told you an hour ago that I'd be ready in a minute!"

Has something like this ever happened to you? Two friends were debating where to spend a beautiful summer day. One said, "Let's go to the roller-skating rink" and the other replied, "Nahh. Nobody goes there anymore because it's too crowded."

A man sobbing at a tombstone was discovered by a stranger repeating, "Why did he heave to die? WHY did he have to die?" The stranger asked sympathetically, "Did you know him well?" and the man replied, "I never met him." The stranger said, "Who was he?" and the man said, "He was my wife's first husband."

One husband who was down in the dumps moaned, "I wish I looked like Mel Gibson." His wife said, "I wouldn't like it if you looked like Mel Gibson." When he asked why not she said, "Because, if you looked like Mel Gibson, I don't think I would love you the way I do now." "I wouldn't care," he said.

A woman came home unexpectedly one day and found her husband–who was obese and totally bald–in bed with another woman. She said, "I have to do that; I'm married to him. But what's your excuse?"

In a discussion about the problems of New York City, a man commented to a friend, "You know, of course, that it's the recent immigrants who are to blame for most of New York's problems." "No, it's the circus clowns" his friend said. "Why the circus clowns?" the man asked. "Why the immigrants?" his friend answered.

A man was very irritated when he was told to move his car. "If this street is off-limits," he told the policeman, "why didn't you tell the drivers of those cars that they couldn't park here?" "They didn't ask," said the cop.

On another occasion, the same man was stopped for speeding. Before the highway patrolman could write him a ticket, his wife said, "It serves you right! You should throw the book at him, officer! He never listens when I tell him to slow down!" The patrolman closed his book and said, "You've been punished enough! Drive on!" As the couple drove away, the husband said, "Thanks sweetie! Your acting talents let me speed whenever I want!"

A teen who had befriended an old man with few visitors decided to pay him an unexpected visit. When he arrived, he was surprised to find the man wearing nothing but a tie. "Why aren't you dressed?" he asked. "Well," said the old man, "I figured I might as well be comfortable, since no one comes to visit me." "So why are you wearing the tie?" the teen asked. "Someone might," was his reply.

One author was tired of hearing people say, "Any idiot can write a best seller." When he heard a friend say it, he snapped, "If that's the case, then why haven't YOU?"

A doctor was annoyed by a call at 3 a.m. from a man

who said his wife had appendicitis. "That's impossible!" the doctor said. "Nobody has two appendixes–and I took your wife's appendix out a year ago." "That's all true," the man admitted, "but a man can have two wives, can't he?"

Another man was dying during a thunderstorm and asked his wife to call a priest. "But we're Jewish!" she said. "I know," he replied, "but I don't want to make the rabbi come out in such weather!"

A man gave up his seat on the bus to a woman and told his companion, "She reminded me of mother." "Because she looks the way your mother did?" his friend asked. "No," he replied, "because of the strap she held in her hand."

Three days after a man started taking a prescription to give him more energy, he wound up more exhausted than ever. "I'm sure it's because of all the running and skipping I've been doing," he told his wife. "What running and skipping?" she asked. "The running and skipping the doctor told me to do," he explained. "He told me to take my medicine two days running and skip the third day."

A naive young woman once became engaged to a heavy gambler. A friend asked her, "Tell me, what do you see in a bum like him?" "He's really a warm, generous person," she explained. "He told me that he put his shirt on a horse that was scratched."

An efficiency expert was mugged and had his car stolen on the same day. He was visited by friends that evening–who were stunned to find him acting cheerful.

When they asked him how he could be so happy, he said, "It's simple. I figured out how to worry as much in half an hour as most people do in weeks."

Excuses for Drivers

The following excuses were written by automobile drivers on accident insurance forms.

I had to drive all over the road before I hit him.

I took one look at my mother-in-law and drove over the embankment.

A tree sprang out of nowhere and hit the front of the car.

I put my head out the window before I noticed it was up.

I was taken by surprise so the accident happened in the back seat.

One driver was infuriated when he bumped the car ahead of him because its driver failed to signal. "Why didn't you signal?" he asked, and the other driver said, "I didn't have to–I always turn here."

A state trooper stopped a speeding driver and asked him why he was going 53 miles an hour when the posted speed limit was 35. The driver said, "Simple–because I'm dyslexic."

Another state trooper asked a man why he had been speeding and was told "Because of sickness." "Are you on your way to the hospital?" the trooper asked. "No, the racetrack," he answered. "Gambling is my sickness!"

Ain't Misbehaving–Unless I'm Caught

There are times when even the shrewdest individual can trip himself up without realizing it. If you wish to avoid doing so, study the following examples well–and keep your foot out of your mouth as much as possible. (Unless of course you're studying Super-Ultra-Advanced Yoga–if so, you could reach Nirvana that way.)

A secretary once insisted that her boss's advances toward her amounted to sexual harassment. Finally she went to her company's lawyer and said, "Last night he seduced me!" The lawyer said, "Can you prove it?" She promised to get proof and left. The next morning she told him, "I now have proof, because last night he seduced me again!"

Later, this woman hit a wealthy actor with a paternity suit and asked him what he was planning to do for the baby. "I'll pay $20,000 a month," he said, "and I'll provide an expensive house for the two of you to live in." "Wonderful!" she said. "Tell me, if I have a miscarriage, can I try again?"

A soldier who had been overseas for two years returned to his wife and the two soon headed for the bedroom to celebrate. When someone knocked on the door the soldier jumped up and said "Is that your husband?" and his wife blurted out, "No, no, he's in Europe."

Two men were undressing in the locker room of a health club when one noticed that the other was wearing pantyhose. "When did you start wearing pantyhose?" he asked. "When my wife found a pair in the glove compartment," he answered.

Could this be an untold Leona Helmsley story? A guest at a fancy hotel was completely shocked to find that her bed contained bedbugs. She complained to the management and checked out. When she got home she found the following letter of apology from the hotel.

"Dear Honored Guest," the letter read. "We offer you our humblest apologies for inconveniencing you in such a manner. We sincerely hope that you will be gracious enough to let us serve you in the future, because we live to make our guests happy." She was very pleased with this special response until she noticed a memo stuck to the back of it. The memo read, "Send this idiot The Bedbug Letter."

A man was dallying with a married woman when she heard someone entering the apartment. "That must be my husband!" she shouted. "Quick, jump out the window!" "But we're on the 13th floor!" The man protested. The woman replied, "There is no time for superstition!"

More Excuses for Kids

If you're an average kid, these excuses ought to come in handy. Haven't you always wanted to find new ways to defend your selfishness and your devotion to sibling rivalry? Wouldn't you like to fend off a parental lecture with a laugh? If so, read on:

"Why did you kick your little brother in the stomach?" one mother asked her little girl. "Because he turned around," she explained.

The same mother asked the same daughter, "Why didn't you notice when the pot boiled over, as I asked you to?" Her precocious daughter quickly replied, "I did notice. It happened at 12:03 p.m."

One snowy day, a little boy's mother scolded him for not sharing the use of his new sled. "I thought I told you to let your little brother use it half the time," she said. "I did," he insisted. "He had it going up the hill and I had it going down."

The same mother caught the same son in the act of slapping his baby brother. "I asked you to try to keep him quiet!" she said. "Why did you slap him?" "What did I have to lose?" he asked. "He was ALREADY bawling his eyes out."

"Every time you misbehave, I get a gray hair!" one mother protested to her little boy. (I'll bet it was the kid above.) His response was, "You must have been a terror when YOU were little! Just look at grandma's hair!"

One first-grade teacher faced the unenviable task of helping all her students on with their galoshes. She had to struggle for a long time to get the galoshes on one little boy's feet, and when at last they were on, he said, "These aren't mine." She struggled just as long to get them off, and then she said, "Whose are they?" "They're my brother's." he said, "but mother makes me wear them."

When to Stop Making the Same Old Excuses

We all hear–and make–the same old excuses over and over again. Excuses such as "I've just never had the opportunity to get ahead" and "There's just too much competition in that field." It's not necessary to keep making such excuses when all you need is to show a little ingenuity, as these individuals did.

Two show salesmen were once sent to the same underdeveloped area to try to drum up sales. The first soon called his boss and said, "I'm coming right back. Everyone here goes barefoot!" The second called and said, "Send me 50 cases of shoes. No one here has any!"

One young man was struggling through a grueling job interview when his interrogator asked him to display some quick thinking. Without hesitation, he threw open the door of the office and told the waiting applicants, "You can leave now. The position has been filled."

One man was outraged when he received his hotel bill because it included a charge for using the hotel's pool. "I didn't use the pool! he protested. The desk clerk explained, "It was there. You could have used it if you wanted to." The man thought quickly and said, "All right, I'll pay the fee. But I'm going to sue you for attacking my wife." "I didn't attack your wife!" the astonished clerk said. Said the man, "She was there..." Laughing, the clerk crossed off the charge.

An office supply salesman peeked hesitantly into the office of a nasty executive and said, "you don't want any supplies, do you? I guess not. I'll be going now." Before he could leave, the executive roared, "That was the WORST selling technique I ever heard in my life. You come back here and I'LL tell you how to sell." The executive lectured the salesman for half an hour. Finally he said, "Now, to give you a little encouragement, I'll place a small order." After the salesman had taken down the order, the executive asked, "Tell me, what technique will you use on your next customer?" Before he dashed out, the salesman said, "The same one I used on you–my technique for tough customers!"

A man who had been looking for an apartment for weeks spotted a man drowning in Central Park. When he recognized the man, and realized that he had a nice apartment, he rushed to his apartment house to rent it. As he walked in the door, he heard the landlord say, "You'll take his apartment? Fine." He looked at the man who had gotten the apartment and said, "How did you get here so fast? Only I saw him drown!" The man said, "Who do you think pushed him in?"

A woman whose son had just gotten married was asked by a friend about the happy couple. "I haven't seen them recently," she said. They don't want me to visit them." Her friend was outraged. "What are you going to do about that?" she asked. "I'm going to wait until they have a child," the woman answered. "I know that a grandmother is always a much more welcome visitor than a mother-in-law!"

Two seminary students were supposed to be praying, but both were distracted by the desire to smoke. One went to see his teacher, returned and said, "I asked him if I could smoke while praying, and he said 'No'." The second said, "Let me go ask." When he returned, he pulled out a cigarette and lit it up. "How did you get permission?" his fellow student asked in amazement. "It had to do with the way I asked him," the student explained. "You asked him if you could smoke while praying, but I asked him if I could pray while smoking."

Two men worked at desks that were side by side and held similar positions, but one always had much more work than the other. Finally the overworked one said, "I don't understand it. How come my desk is always piled with papers and yours is practically empty?" The other man said, "Whenever I get a complicated assignment, I attach a memo to it that says, 'Send this to Smith.' I figured that in a company this size there must be someone named Smith–and it's worked out well because none on the assignments ever come back to me." "ARRRGGGH!" his colleague growled. "I'M SMITH!"

A little boy wanted to stay over at his friend's house, so he asked his mother, "Can I stay over at Frankie's house? His mother said that if it's all right with you, it's all right with her." His mother agreed to his request. A short while later, after Frankie had gotten a call from his friend, he asked his mother, "Is it all right if Bobby stays over tonight? His mother said that if it's all right with you, it's all right with her"–and his mother, of course, agreed to his request!

A worried parent hadn't heard from his son–who was away at college–for a long time. In order to get an immediate response, he wrote him a letter that ended with: I want you to use the $100 I've enclosed for something very special"–but he didn't enclose the money!

More Assorted Excuses

Sometimes the best way to come up with a good excuse is to seek out a new and different twist to the situation. Study these stories carefully and you will gain a new appreciation for offbeat thinking.

A heavy drinker who spent night after night at his favorite bar was surprised one evening when his wife showed up. "You should be ashamed of yourself!" she said. "You're here every night enjoying drinks when you could be doing something serious." Her husband said, "Have a drink with me!" She said, "I will not! You know I don't drink!" He said, "Come on, just this once." "All right, just this once," she answered, and he ordered a whiskey for her. When it arrived, she took just one sip and spat it out. "UGH!" she said, "This tastes TERRIBLE!" "You see?" he said. "And you thought I was having a good time!"

A boy selling papers called out, "BIG SWINDLE! THIRTY-NINE VICTIMS SO FAR!" A man who was passing bought a paper and scanned its pages quickly. "I don't see anything about a big swindle here," he said. "Where is it mentioned?" The boy just called out, "BIG SWINDLE! FORTY VICTIMS SO FAR!"

A minister felt tempted to play golf on Sunday and decided to sneak off and play a round by himself. God and an angel saw him playing, and the angel said, "He deserves to be punished. "I'm going to punish him right now," God said. Watch this!" As soon as the minister hit his golf ball, God made it fly around a tree three times, roll up and down four hills, fly into the air and finally drop into the hole! "Do You call that punishment?" the angel asked. "Yes," said God, "who can he tell?"

A woman mailing a package at the post office was told, "This is too heavy–you'll have to put more stamps on it." She said, "More stamps will only make it heavier!"

The manger of a big department store was strolling near a counter one day when he heard a clerk say, "We haven't had any for a while, and I have no idea when we'll be getting any more." Shocked, he took the clerk aside and said, "Don't EVER tell any customers that something isn't available and can't be obtained. Always tell them that we'll do everything we can to get them anything they want. Now, what did that customer want?" "She wanted to know if I thought it would rain soon," the clerk replied.

A manager told a joke at an office party that made all his employees laugh except one. The employee was asked why she didn't laughed, and she said, "I don't have to. I'm leaving on Friday."

A thief found a pocketbook stuffed with money in a big department store and brought it to the store's Lost and Found Department. On the way out, he picked a store employee's pocket and was caught in the act. "I don't understand it," the employee said. "Why did you return the pocketbook and then try to rob me?" "YOU don't understand," the thief replied. "Returning the pocketbook was a good deed, but robbing you was a *business* venture."

A young man who had just started working as an optometrist's assistant asked his boss, "How much do the glasses cost?" "The prices vary from time to time," said the optometrist. "Why is that?" his assistant asked. "It's like this," his boss said. "When a customer asks how much a pair of glasses are, you say, "They're $40.' If the customer doesn't flinch, you say, 'I meant the frames are $40. The lenses are another $40.' And if the customer still doesn't flinch, you say, 'Each'!"

A man was walking down the street minding his own business when a stranger started hitting him and shouting, "Harry, you stink! Take this, Harry! You're a creep, Harry!" "You've got the wrong man!" the innocent victim said. The stranger kept hitting him and said, "What do you care what I do to Harry?"

A doctor whose son was in medical school went on a brief vacation and left his son in charge of his office. When he came back, his son said proudly, "I cured one of your patients, Dad! The woman who was your patient for the last 10 years!" "Idiot!" said his father, "She was putting you through medical school!"

From the moment a long bus trip began, the bus driver was pestered by a woman who said, "Tell me when we get to Main Street! Don't forget to tell me when we get to Main Street!" The bus driver promised he wouldn't forget and the woman fell asleep. Later on, the driver was horrified when he realized that he had forgotten to tell the woman when the bus arrived at Main Street. Although he had gone a long way past it, he turned the bus around and drove back. Then he woke her up and said, "Here we are." We're at Main Street." Without making a move to get off, she said, "Oh, good! My doctor told me to take my medication when I got to Main Street."

Soldiers were gathered in a bar that was constantly being bombed, and one was boasting about his great courage. When a bomb fell nearby, all the soldiers stayed seated except the one who had been boasting. He flung himself to the floor. When he got up and faced his grinning comrades, he said, "What's the matter? Were you too frightened to move?"

A hunter was exploring in the jungle when he encountered a lion. There was nowhere he could run, so he began to pray. When he looked up, he saw that the lion was also praying. The lion said to him, "I don't know what you're doing, but I'm saying grace."

A very spoiled girl once whined to her boyfriend, "Why don't you get me a mink coat? You know I'm terribly cold." "That's why!" he said.

When a man answered questions about his parents on a medical insurance form, he couldn't bring himself to state that his father had been hung. At last he wrote, "He died on-stage at a well-attended public event when the platform gave way."

At a gala performance by a popular singer, his attention was caught by an old woman in the first row. Every time he took center stage, she would say, "Wonderful! That is so wonderful!" The singer was deeply touched by her comments and decided to thank her after the show. He went up to her and said, "I really appreciate the nice things you said about my singing. Which song did you like best?" "Songs? What songs?" she said. "I didn't pay much attention to your singing. But whenever they turned that big spotlight on you, and I felt heat on my back easing my arthritis–that was so wonderful!"

A millionaire eating in a fancy restaurant asked his waiter, "What was the biggest tip you ever got?" "$100," the waiter said. "Here is $100," the millionaire said. "I don't want anyone to be a bigger tipper than I am. Now, tell me, who gave you the $100 tip?" "You did," the waiter said.

A lion was stalking through the jungle asking every animal he met, "Who's the King of Beasts?" All the animals answered, "You are, lion, you are." When he met an elephant and asked him the question, the elephant picked him up and threw him into the air. As the lion got up and patted his fur, he said, "Just because you don't know the answer, you don't have to get mad!"

"Why won't you go out with me?" whined a young man to a reluctant girl. "You know that I'd go to the ends of the earth for you!" "I believe that," she said, "but how do I know you would stay there?"

An English professor told her class, "To remember the poet Bobby Burns, picture an English policeman–a bobby–surrounded by flames." One of her students said, "But that could also mean Robert Browning!"

Excuses That Backfired

A man who felt ill heard about a doctor who charged much less for a second visit than he did for the first. He walked into his office and said, Here I am for my second visit"–and the doctor said, "Keep doing what I told you to do last time."

A collector of antiques was stunned when he noticed a cat drinking from a priceless porcelain bowl. Positive that the store owner had no idea of its value, he said to him, "I love the cat you have here. Would you mind selling him to me?" The owner agreed and accepted $30 for the cat. As soon as the collector had completed the transaction, he said, "Why don't I take his drinking bowl with me? He must be used to drinking out of it." "No, you can't have it," the owner said. "Why not?" the collector said. "It doesn't look very valuable." "It's like this," the owner said. "I've sold 10 cats with that bowl already."

A notorious gangster was on trial for murder and, afraid of going to the electric chair, he begged one of the jurors, "Please, please do me a favor–ask that I be given *life*." The juror agreed, and that was the verdict–a life sentence. The gangster stopped to thank the juror, and she said, "I was glad to be of help. The other jurors were in favor of letting you go free, but I held out for life."

A parent, trying to be helpful, told her 5-year-old, "You've got your shoes on the wrong feet!" Her little boy burst into tears and said, "These are the only feet I have!"

An old woman broke her leg and was told by her doctor not to climb any stairs until the cast was taken off.

When it was finally removed, she shouted, "Hallelujah! Whoopee! I'm so happy!" The doctor said, "You must have been relieved to get that itchy cast off." "It's not that, doctor," she said. "I just got so sick and tired of climbing up and down the drainpipe!"

A proud car owner who had just paid $10,000 for his car spotted a friend in a beat-up vehicle and couldn't resist teasing him. He drove up alongside and said, "What's that rattling sound coming from your car?" Said his friend, "It's the $9,500 jingling in my pocket."

One man complained to a friend, "I can't stand the smell in my apartment! My wife is taking care of a friend's ferrets, my son bought three hamsters and my brother just brought over his dogs!" "Why don't you open a window?" his friend suggested. "What?" he said, "and let my four parrots escape?"

A governor was making an inspection tour through a jail, asking prisoners why they were there. All of them said they had been framed, except for one man who said, "I won't make any excuses. I was sent here because I was guilty." The governor said, "Pardon this man at once, before he corrupts all the innocent people!"

On Visiting Day at his young son's elementary school, a father watched as his son did an arithmetic problem. "How much is six and six?" the teacher asked. "Eight," the little boy said. "That is incorrect," said the teacher. "Okay, so he was wrong," his father said. "But he only missed it by one!"

In a nursing home, an old woman who had little money wanted some cigarettes and decided to try bartering for them. She unraveled an old blanket she owned until she had enough wool to knit a pair of socks, and traded the socks for a carton of cigarettes. She kept doing this until she only had enough wool left for one sock, and then decided to see if anyone would want just one. The same old woman who had "bought" all her other socks bought the last one, and the knitter asked her what she wanted with one sock. "Unraveling the sock will give me just enough wool to finish the blanket I've been knitting," she said.

A sociologist decided to try an experiment. She abandoned one car on a street in New York and another on a street in Los Angeles. After a few days, the car in New York was almost completely destroyed–and the car in Los Angeles was hardly touched. The sociologist, a native New Yorker, came to this conclusion: "People in New York are neater!"

An executive beginning a business trip was very irritated when he missed his plane by a single minute. He started cursing, and a woman standing nearby said, "Now, now, there's no excuse for that! You're acting as though you missed it by a whole hour!"

A vagrant was caught going through garbage cans in front of a row of identical houses. "What do you think you're doing, going through my garbage?" he was asked. "It's not the way it looks," the vagrant said. "I just moved into one of these houses to stay with my brother. Then I went for walk and got confused about which one was his–so I was looking for our garbage!"

A well-known boxer, notorious for insulting his opponents, was driving one day when his car was hit from behind. The other driver immediately jumped out and started shouting at him, but the boxer didn't say a word. After the other driver had exhausted his anger, he drove off and the boxer calmly got back into his car. The friend with him asked, "Why didn't you talk back to that man?" "If you insulted Pavarotti, would you expect him to sing an aria?" the boxer replied.

A little boy didn't want to stop watching a baseball game on television until his mother said she would keep watching it for him. The next morning he asked her, "What was the final score?" "Four to one," she said. "And who won?" he asked. "The team that got four," she said.

On Mother's Day, one dutiful son sent his mother a very expensive coat. When she called to thank him, she said, "I hope you didn't spend too much money on that coat," and he replied, "No, I didn't do that. It was only $50. A few weeks later she called him and said, "Send me 10 more coats. I sold the one you sent me for $75!"

At the beginning of a classical concert, the world-famous conductor looked over the audience and thought, "This doesn't look like a very sophisticated group. So, instead of having the orchestra play the obscure selection in the program, I'll have them play something more familiar." After the concert ended, a member of the audience approached the conductor and said, "I want to hear the selection you didn't conduct. I won't be satisfied until I hear it." The conductor was delighted. "You're a true music lover!" he said. "I'll have the orchestra play it just for you." He did so, and then asked the man, "What did you think?" "That was the first time I ever heard it," the man said. "And I didn't like it!"

"I wish I had 10 clients like you," a salesman said to an irritating client. Why is that?" he asked. "Because I *have* a hundred!" he said.

When Aristotle Onassis died, a man discovered a friend crying over a paper that reported his death. He asked, "Why are you crying? Were you related to him?" "No," the man sobbed, "that's why I'm crying!"

An old woman got on a crowded train for a long journey and found another woman, about her age, stretched out across two seats. Wanting a seat, and wanting to be as diplomatic as possible about getting it, she thought carefully. At last she nudged the woman, got her to sit up, and sat down next to her, saying, "I haven't seen you since your wedding! What's been going on since then?"

Wise Guy (and Gal) Excuses

If you're a wise guy (or gal) at heart...or, you always wanted to be one, but didn't know how to get started...these are just for you!

A soldier who had been pressured to join the Army against his will soon found that volunteering for anything was a big mistake. He vowed to himself that he would never volunteer for any distasteful chore if he could help it. One day his sergeant asked, "Does anyone here know shorthand?" and since it sounded like a straightforward question–and he knew shorthand–the soldier said, "Yes. I do." "OK," the sergeant said, "report to the kitchen–we're short-handed on dishwashers!"

An executive dictated a personal letter to his secretary (who had a crush on him) and then said, "Type it up." When he read it over, he said, "You left out 'I Love You' at the end." "I thought you had stopped dictating," said the secretary.

A Romeo who was reluctant to take 'no' for an answer, and had heard every excuse in the book (this book, of course), escorted a girl to her apartment and said, "Let me come in." "You can't come in," she replied. "Why?" he sneered, "Because your roommate's sleeping?" "No," she said seductively, "because she's awake."

"My husband is so romantic," one long-married friend told another. "He says 'I Love You' all the time–does yours?" "No," her friend replied. "But when you make beautiful music together, who needs words?"

"You must apologize to your teacher for what you said to her," said Dr. Alpern, a principal, to a misbehaving student. "You know, Dr. Alpern," said the student, "there are times when an apology is worse than an insult." "How can that be?" asked the principal. "Wait until the parent-teacher luncheon tomorrow and I'll show you," the boy said. The next day, when the principal was seated next to his wife, the boy came up behind him and pinched his rear end. Outraged, Dr. Alpern jumped up and said "How dare you do such a thing to me!" "I'm very sorry, sir," said the boy, "but I thought you were Mrs. Alpern."

When an extremely dignified woman heard bad language from the workmen repairing her house, she complained to their foreman about it. The foreman told them about the complaint and said, "What did you say? What happened?" "We didn't say anything wrong," one workman said. "I was on top of the ladder and Jimmy was at the bottom when I accidentally dropped a red-hot rivet down his neck. Then he just looked up at me and said, 'Be more careful next time, Bill'."

A judge who had dismissed a youth's case because it was his first offense told him, "Don't hang around bums and loafers any more!" "I won't!" he said, "You won't see me in front of you again!"

A certain determined Romeo propositioned a girl who said, "I'd like to, but I know I'd hate myself in the morning." "So sleep late!" he said.

The same determined wolf asked a waitress for her

phone number and she said, "It's in the phone book." He then asked her for her name, and she said, "That's in the phone book, too."

A girl who had just gotten engaged was dying to mention in to her co-workers, but no one noticed her ring. At last she said, "It's so hot in here I think I'll take off my new ring."

A bar patron called the bartender over one day and said, "If you give me another drink on the house, I'll tell you a surefire way to sell twice as much liquor as you do now." The bartender gave him a drink and said, "How?" "Fill up the glasses," he said.

Double Excuses

Every expert excuse-maker occasionally finds it necessary to have two excuses on hand–one for himself and one for other people. A handy list for those occasions when you need double excuses follows.

THE EXCUSE YOU MAKE TO OTHERS	THE EXCUSE YOU MAKE TO YOURSELF	THE TRUTH
You're only young once!	I really wanted to do it.	Everybody else was doing it.
I didn't eat it.	I was really hungry.	I wanted to stuff my face.
I don't have time to see it.	I heard that it's very good.	If I saw it, I'd have nightmares.
My friend talked me into seeing Disneyworld again.	I heard that the natives in that country are arrogant.	I'm just a hick at heart.
I'm burned out from too much dating.	She's not my type.	She turned me down.
I don't have time.	I don't have time.	I don't have the talent.

I work so hard that I can't eat right.	It's because of my metabolism.	I eat too much.
I had a moment of weakness.	I'm entitled to indulge myself occasionally.	I'm weak.
It's not right to have someone else do your homework for you.	It's best that I let my son work it out for himself.	I have no idea how to do those geometry problems.
The kids insisted.	I wanted the kids to experience Disneyland while they were still small.	*I* really wanted to go.(After all, how much can two 6-month-olds absorb?)
The rock-climbing class was filled.	I'm going to get into better shape before I sign up.	I'm lazy, and scared stiff at the *thought* of rock-climbing!
I would never wear anything as cheap-looking as that.	That's too cheap-looking even for me.	I couldn't begin to get into that outfit.
I have another party to go to.	I have better things to do.	I'm going to go home and change the cat's litter.
I heard that she's pushy.	She acts too intimidating.	I don't have the nerve to talk to her.

I only watch PBS.

I only watch intellectual shows.

I wonder what Vanna will wear tonight.

"You, Me and Him" Game

The "You, Me and Him" Game is a matter of making excuses by using carefully selected adjectives. Describing one trait shared by three different people means using three entirely different adjectives or descriptions. Choosing the right adjective means determining whether your subject is you–me–or him. For example:

I'M a woman of the world. *YOU'RE* a bit promiscuous. *SHE'S* a slut.

I'M a ladies' man. *YOU'RE* a playboy. *HE'S* a callous, insensitive bastard.

I'M a smart shopper. *YOU'RE* a little tight-fisted. *HE'S* very stingy.

I know how to relax. *YOU* move too leisurely. *HE'S* lazy.

I know how to have a good time. *YOU'RE* extravagant. *HE* throws his money away.

I'M ahead of my time. *YOU'RE* eccentric. *HE'S* weird.

I'M a genius. *YOU'RE* bright. *HE'S* intelligent.

I learn a lot from traveling. *YOUR* wanderings are amusing. *HE* ought to settle down.

I'M too intelligent to hold a regular job. *YOU* ought to apply yourself more. *HE* can't get it together.

MY children are high-spirited. *YOUR* children are mischievous. *HER* children are spoiled brats.

MY operation was torture. *YOUR* operation was minor. *HER* operation was nothing.

MY car accident was traumatic. *YOUR* accident was dramatic. *HIS* car accident was a fender-bender.

MY burglary was the crime of the century. *YOUR* burglary was a shame. *HIS* burglary was trivial.

I'M an actor. *YOU'RE* on the fringes of show business. *HE'S* a waiter.

MY girlfriend is gorgeous. *YOUR* girlfriend is attractive. *HIS* girlfriend is cheap-looking.

I'M a Renaissance man. *YOU'RE* a jack-of-all-trades. *HE* has no idea what he wants to do.

I attended the College of Hard Knocks. *YOU'RE* partially educated. *HE'S* a drop-out.

MY boyfriend is handsome. *YOUR* boyfriend is attractive. *HER* boyfriend is too good-looking.

An anecdote that focuses on the basic principle of the You, Me and Him Game involves a conversation between a middle-aged mother and one of her old friends. Her old friend asks, "Tell me, how are your son and his new bride getting along?" "Terribly!" was the reply. "The woman my son made the mistake of marrying forces him to bring her breakfast in bed every morning. She also forced him to get a maid because she's too lazy to clean.

To top it off, she forces him to taker her to dinner every night because she doesn't like to cook!"

Her friend said, "Well, how are your daughter and her new husband getting along?" "Wonderfully!" she replied. "Her husband is an absolute angel! He brings her breakfast in bed each and every morning! He insisted on getting her a maid so she doesn't have to clean! And, every night, he takes her out to dinner!"

Classic Excuses Revisited

Everyone has heard hundreds of classic excuses. They include the following:

1. I have a headache.
2. I have a stomach ache.
3. I have to work late at the office.
4. I'm too old.
5. I'm too young.
6. Everyone will stare at me.
7. No one will look at me.
8. I could never go alone.
9. I never did it before.
10. I'm tired of doing it.

Triumphing over creaky excuses such as these means trying new approaches. Don't say you're afraid to try anything new–keep reading!

When you're with someone who has resisted your advances many times by using phony-sounding excuses (the nerve of him/her!) try this: Ask your date, "Do you have a headache, a stomach ache, a cold, a fever, heat rash or whiplash?" When you get a response– which will almost certainly be a puzzled "No"–say, "GOTCHA!" and proceed from there.

If you're an old man who has just married a young girl and a buttinsky relative exclaims, "The age difference could be fatal!" reply, "If she dies, she dies!"

If you're a gold-digger who is working hard on a guy loaded with moolah, this excuse should come in handy. The next time some jealous female friend sneers, "Isn't he too old to be considered eligible?" snap, "He's too eligible to be considered old!"

One woman who was sick and tired of hearing people say that singles aren't supposed to live well, took an important step towards making herself feel important. She walked into a bakery, ordered a cake in the shape of the letter "l" and gave the baker very specific instructions. She said, "I want it to have pink icing on the sides, forming precise loops, and blue rosettes circling the top. It must have three distinct layers–chocolate, strawberry and marble." The baker promised her that he would follow her instructions precisely and told her the cake would be ready in a week. A week later she returned and said, "I told you to make it in the shape of a curlicued 'l' and you made it in the shape of a regular 'l'." He promised he would change it and told her to come back in another week. When she returned, she expressed her satisfaction and the baker said, "Shall I wrap it up now?" She answered, "No, thank you. I'll eat it here."

A mother training her child to recognize phony excuses saw an opening one night when her daughter asked, "Mommy, do all fairy tales start with 'Once upon a time'?" "No," her mother replied, "some start with, I'll have to work very late tonight'."

Up-to-the-Minute Excuses

These days you can't help bumping into people who claim they were once kidnapped by space aliens (to excuse a mysterious weekend disappearance). I have my suspicions about these individuals, and I'd say the odds are good that many of them spent their "lost weekends" at the Hot Sheet Hotel, in the arms of someone other than Morpheus.

Utilizing such an excuse yourself is simple, and a good idea for more reasons than one. Not only will people swallow such bilge-water whole, you might also get a best-seller from your spurious story.

If you decide to go this route, please keep in mind the following rules:

1. Aliens never seem to kidnap earthlings for any reason other than to run medical experiments on them. Tabloid claims about hybrid offspring are to the contrary. Don't get cute and embellish your tacky tale with details about voluptuous space maidens or bug-eyed monsters. Missing out on a chance to outdo Edgar Rice Burroughs is no fun, I know, but who are you to buck hallowed tradition?
2. Don't bother providing any solid "proof." No one ever has, but their crack-brained chronicles are believed just the same. Don't bother throwing a frisbee in the air above your camera, or taking some blurry snapshots of your sister in her Halloween costume from 50 feet away. Just say that you saw bright lights appearing from nowhere, and that you forgot all about the encounter until the moment you got a fat, juicy contract from the *National*

Enquirer.

Other helpful modern excuses include:

I lost the software disc with your number on it. If it will make your feel any better, I lost all my recipes for chocolate pickle quiche at the same time!

Last time I got this turned on, my smoke alarm sprinklers went off and drenched me! I know it's going to take a while before I can forget the trauma and function normally again.

I fast-forwarded through *The Exorcist* recently, and the sudden avalanche of subliminal horrors sent me to a sanatorium–where I couldn't use the phone.

Last week I flew to London on the Concorde in only a few hours–but, unfortunately, I had to wait five days until my luggage arrived!

Improvising Excuses

Now that you have acquired a solid foundation of classic and modern excuses, it's time to think about going solo. After all, panic can cause memorized material to evaporate from your brain just as water does from a sauna slab. An even better reason for absorbing the essentials of successful excuse-concocting–this will count as one-third of your final grade.

BASIC RULES FOR ALIBI INVENTING

1. When fate forces you to fib your way out of some unpleasantness, NEVER USE THE SAME EXCUSE ON THE SAME PERSON TWICE IN A ROW. This may seem obvious, but neglecting this simple but vital rule has halted many an individual at the gateway to Fibbing for Fun and Profit. One excuse, no matter how believable it may sound at first, can never be stretched to deflect two heapings of wrath. Don't be lazy, keep track of your lying. Keep a list if you have to. Just do not, for example, tell your teacher on two consecutive days that your dog ate your homework. Strangely, she will blame–not the dog–but you. And why? Because you failed to develop your imagination as well as you should be developing your deltoids. (I don't have time at the moment to listen to your excuses about why you aren't. Until I need them for the sequel to this book, kindly keep them to yourself.) Where was I? Oh, yes. Keep in mind that your teachers have heard every excuse known to man(and woman) relating to "Why I Didn't Do My Homework." When it comes to improvising excuses that will melt their crabby little hearts, focus on these three words: Drastic Is Best. *Drastic*. As in, "I didn't have time to do

my homework because I was performing CPR on a neighbor until the ambulance came." If your teacher doesn't believe your little tale, you may triumph after all–when she gives you an "A" for Creative Writing.

2. Never say, "This time it wasn't my fault, honestly." This shows VERY POOR FORM. Remember ex-President Nixon's infamous announcement, "I am not a crook." He mad the fatal mistake(and boy, was it fatal) of actually implying that he was honest. HONEST PEOPLE DO NOT *SAY* (OR EVEN SUGGEST) THAT THEY ARE HONEST. Which is convenient for people who aren't strictly honest, because it means they don't have to lie about their deficiency. Which means they can devote all their energies to getting away with as much as possible and don't have to waste energy on fabricating falsehoods. Which gives you one less thing to worry about when you're up to no good. Now that we're back on the subject, remember this, also: NOTHING IS *EVER* YOUR FAULT. It may be your brother's fault, it may be your sister's fault, it may be the fault of sunspots or your horoscope, but IT IS NEVER YOUR FAULT. Making excuses means never having to say, "I'm sorry, it was my fault." I have never heard of one man-made major disaster that actually turned out to be somebody's fault. It may have been an "accident," it may have been a "minor miscalculation," but it certainly wasn't anybody's actual FAULT. The tobacco companies swear that their product has very little to do with the ARMY of cancer patients in this country. I've heard that some people actually believe it. If people can believe that, then surely people exist who will believe anything YOU say.

3. Always get your story straight ahead of time. It's often necessary to make excuses in the company of one or

more companions in the same boat. On such occasions, put your heads together and settle on the most plausible-sounding possibility IN TIME. Don't be like the four boys who arrived at school long after their all-important mid-term test had started. They offered the joint excuse that they'd gotten a flat tire. After telling them to take widely separated seats, their teacher said, "All right, here's your first question. Which tire was it?"

4. Handle every little detail, however small. If you don't, you will wind up like the lad with the almost perfect absence note. The note he handed his teacher read, "Johnny was absent yesterday because he had a cold. (signed) My father."

5. If all else fails, try confusing them. Here's an example of a confusing excuse: "I'm late because I had to walk all the way here propelling my bicycle–I didn't have time to get on."

6. Above all, know when to stop elaborating on an excuse. Just being on a roll doesn't make you a hot dog.

Reversing Excuses

For many excuses, there is an equal and opposite excuse. For example, if someone says to you, "What's your excuse for always leaving the toilet seat up?" you can say, "What's YOUR excuse for always leaving it DOWN?" If someone asks, "Why did you keep me waiting so long while you yakked with your buddy?" explain, "He just couldn't stop listening." And if someone catches you lying about the outcome of the (ridiculously one-sided) fight you were in, and says, "Oh, really–YOU scared HIM?" say this: "Yes, he was TREMENDOUSLY scared–he thought he killed me."

One classic reversed excuse came from a highway patrolman, when he explained why he flung himself from his moving motorcycle: "A speeding vehicle took off so fast before me that I thought I was standing still–so I got off to check."

A Double Reversed Excuse was created when an overconfident student made a bet with a friend. He said, "I'll bet I can answer any question you ask about birds–and I'll bet you can't do the reverse." His friend said, "I accept the bet–and furthermore, let's say that if you can't answer a question that I can, you have to pay me $10. And, if I can't answer a question that you can, I only have to pay you $5." The first student agreed and the second asked, "What has six eyes, pink-and-purple wings and flies upside down?" The first student said, "I don't know. Here's your $10." The second one said, "I don't know, either. Here's your $5."

Hourly Excuses

I'm sure that there is someone in your life whom you would rather not see again. In fact, I'm sure that there are several people in your life whom you would love to stash on board the next slow boat to China. This is probably not likely to occur (a terrible shame, isn't it?) but I have a solution that is ALMOST as good.

Let us say that you are an executive who would rather not see a stream of individuals–business acquaintances–if you can possibly avoid it. (Most executives feel this way, oddly enough.) If such is the case with you, you can enjoy a world of new freedom by using these hour-by-hour excuses (it's expected in business).

SAMPLE EXCUSES AND THEIR TRANSLATIONS

Employers, tell your secretary to inform callers that:

9 a.m. He's not in yet. He was working late last night.
TRANSLATION: He has a hangover.

10 a.m. He just got in.
TRANSLATION: He can't function before he has his morning coffee.

11 a.m. He's in a meeting.
TRANSLATION: He and his office mates are comparing notes on the party they both attended last night–"I danced on the table? Really? And I still had my tie on? At least I kept some shred of dignity... My tie was *ALL* I had on???"

12 p.m. He went to lunch.
TRANSLATION: He's drinking his lunch.

1 p.m. He's not back from lunch yet. He had a very important appointment.
TRANSLATION: He had to go see a doctor about his frequent blackouts.

2 p.m. He just stepped out.
TRANSLATION: He's in the john.

3 p.m. He's busy with an interview right now.

TRANSLATION: He went on an interview for a new job. Since his boss found out about his drinking problem, his days at this company are numbered.

4 p.m. He's on the phone with the CEO of the company.
TRANSLATION: He was put on hold by the CEO.

5 p.m. He's gone for the day.
TRANSLATION: He successfully avoided you for another day!

Now let us suppose that you are a housewife with a similar problem. (Go get a sex change. I'll wait.) Let us further suppose the people you wish to avoid whenever possible are your in-laws. Luckily for you, I have some wonderful tailor made excuses for dodging your miserable in-laws (particularly your crummy mother-in-law) when they call. These are excuses to supply on those sad occasions (hopefully infrequent) when you are actually cornered by one or more of them and have to explain why you didn't answer the phone when they called–and called–and called.

HOUSEWIVES' HOUR-BY-HOUR EXCUSES (AN ASSORTMENT)

8 a.m. I was busy running the blender to make breakfast for your darling son.
TRANSLATION: I was asleep. (You trained her darling son to eat breakfast in a coffee shop every morning like everyone else.)

10 a.m. I was vacuuming.
TRANSLATION: I was still asleep.

12 p.m. I was making your darling son lunch.
TRANSLATION: What do you think? (HINT: See earlier note about breakfast.)

2 p.m. I was taking a cold shower quickly, so I could begin baking pies for your darling son as soon as possible.
TRANSLATION: I was taking a hot bath slowly, to kill time before calling the pizza place for supper.

4 p.m. The children were shouting.
TRANSLATION: The children were shouting, "It's your turn to do the cleaning!" "No, it's your turn!" Because I have them well-trained. Cleaning is always done by one of the kids–never by me!

6 p.m. I was busy making supper from scratch for your darling...
TRANSLATION: Oh, You've heard this one before.

Nothing but the Truth

Strange as it may seem, it IS possible to go through life without ever making excuses. (It's just not as much fun.) There are a variety of ways to do this. You could try the "The Best Excuse Is a Fast Excuse" defense practiced by telephone switchboard operators. They use it by answering the phone with "Hello, wouldyoumindholdingforonesecond?Thank you. If you can talk fast enough to say, "Yes, I do mind" to such people before they drop you into "hold limbo" once again, you may have a great career ahead of you as a radio pitchman or possibly a used car salesman.

Then there is the Straightforward Method of Excuse-Making (which is also know as the Suicidal Method). This method involves using the REAL REASON for something in place of an excuse. For example, one boss asked his employees, "How come no one is ever working when I walk in?" and one straightforward employee (now an ex-employee) said, "It's because of those rubber heels you wear."

Another way of bypassing excuse-making is what I call the Dingbat Answer. (I named it after Edith Bunker.) A friend of mine once called a tourist bureau to ask about tours to New England–and was put on hold for a long, long time by a puzzled employee. When she returned to the phone at last, she said, "Sorry, I couldn't find anything for you. I never heard of a state called New England."

Doin' the Twist

The best excuses are the ones that feature unexpected, original twists. Such excuses can confuse even the most astute questioner. To create such excuses, it helps to keep in mind something poet Emily Dickinson once said: "Tell all the truth/but tell it slant." What follows is the Hall of Fame for excuses with a twist.

A couple was deciding on a name for their new baby, and steadily shooting down each other's suggestions. Eventually the husband said, "If it's a boy, how about Matthew?" "Not Matthew!" his wife said. These days every Tom, Dick and Harry is named Matthew!"

The best excuse for being egotistical was created by Prime Minister Golda Meir, who said, "Don't be so humble–you're not that great."

A golf expert took a friend to a golf course for the first time and told him, "Hit the ball as close to the flag as you can." They played 18 holes together and when they finished, the golf expert said, "Don't feel bad about never getting the ball into a hole–that takes time." His friend said, "You never told me to try getting it *IN*!"

As a special favor, a highly successful business consultant agreed to attend a special conference in Canada. It was freezing when he arrived, and he said to a colleague, "Oh, how I wish I were back in New York now!" "Why?" his colleague asked, "It's cold there, too." "I know," he replied, "but if I were back in New York now, I'd be at my house in Florida!"

Two men were discussing their recent business disasters and one said, "Last week, my warehouse burned to the ground!" The other said, "That's nothing, my factory was flooded!" The first said, "I want to ask you a question. How do you cause a flood?"

A wrestler preparing for a bout on television told all his friends and relatives that he was positive he would win. Later, when he lost, they asked him what had gone wrong. He said, "I don't understand how I could have lost–I won every rehearsal!"

When it took one Manhattan restaurant patron 45 minutes to find a parking spot near the restaurant, he asked its owner, "Why don't you get a parking lot?" The owner said, "Are you kidding? If I could get a parking lot, I wouldn't need a restaurant!"

Two young men were hitchhiking in a remote part of France when they were invited to stay with a widowed countess at her castle. A few months later, one of them said to the other, "Tell me...did you sleep with the countess?" His friend admitted that he had. "And did you give her my name and address?" His friend admitted that he had done that, too. After confessing, the friend said, "Why do you ask?" "Because I just received a letter from her lawyer," he said. "She left me the castle!"

While on his Las Vegas honeymoon, a man who had never gambled before lost almost all of the money that he had brought. When all he had left was $2, he went back to their hotel room and told his wife they had to leave. He added, "While you're packing, I might as well bet the last $2 and see what happens." He went back to the casino, put a quarter in the slot machine and won

$50. Then he went to the craps table and won $50,000! He felt so lucky that he bet it all–and lost. When he returned to the room, his wife asked, "What happened?" and he said, "I lost the $2."

A high school girl who had a reputation for being "easy" announced in school that she was pregnant and was planning to seek child support from the father. One of her male classmates shouted, "It wasn't me–I never touched her!" The others chimed in, "Neither did I...I never went near her...She wouldn't even kiss me" and so on, until they had all spoken. "Thanks, guys!" the girl said. "I was hoping to ditch my reputation, and you've confirmed that it's meaningless. As you've probably guessed–I'm NOT pregnant!"

A man walked into a florist shop and said, "You don't have any rubber plants, do you?" The florist said, "No, we just ran out of them. How about some African violets?" The man said, "No, I have to get rubber plants, because they're what I promised my girlfriend I'd water while she was away."

A couple was invited to visit a poultry farm and they were taken separately to see different parts of it. The guide showing the wife around pointed to a rooster and said, "See that bird? He does his duty by the chickens six times a day." The wife said, "Tell my husband that." He went to tell her husband, and he said, "Does he do it with one single chicken?" The poultry expert said, "No, with six different chickens." The husband said,"Tell my wife that."

Another neglected wife was watching a romantic movie with her husband, and when the lead actors kissed, said, "Why don't you do that?" He said, "I don't even know that actress."

An interviewer was visiting the home of a renowned tycoon when he spotted three plaques on the wall. He asked, "How did you happen to get three awards for public service?" The tycoon said, "I was given the first because I had never gotten one. I was given the second because I had already been given one. And I got the third because I had already gotten two."

A street performer who had performed trick after trick for over half an hour passed the hat and got it back without a penny in it. He looked at the empty hat and said, "Thank goodness!" His friend said, "Why did you say 'Thank goodness' about an empty hat?" He said, "Why? Because with a crowd as poor as that, I was lucky to get my hat back."

A woman of 30 was tired of being asked why she was married to a man of 60. Finally, she started answering in this manner: "When he was 40, I was 10, and he was four times my age. When I was 15, he was 45, and he was three times my age. Right now he's twice my age, so before long we ought to be the same age!"

A tailor who had taken months to make a custom-made suit was asked, "Why does it take you so long to make one suit? God made the world in only six days." "True," said the tailor, "but look at the shape it's in!"

A man living in a slum said to his friend, "If I were Donald Trump, I would move here. Then I'd be certain of living forever." "What makes you say that?" his friend asked. "Because," he explained, "no rich man has ever died here."

Big businessman Gary Brodsky loves the following joke: A witness testifying in a court case was interrupted by the defense lawyer every time he started a sentence with "I think..." "Don't start with 'I think'," the lawyer said. "We want to hear facts, not opinions." "I'm sorry, sir," the witness said, "but I can't speak without thinking. I'm not a lawyer."

A professional boxer kept saying to his manager, "I want to fight Marty the Mangler! I want to fight Marty the Mangler!" And his manager kept telling him, "YOU are Marty the Mangler!"

A man bought a suit from a store that had a sign in the window stating, "Our middle name is quality." He brought it back and said, "This is a mess! How can your middle name be quality?" "It's a fact," the store owner insisted. "Unfortunately, our first name is 'lousy'!"

Survivors gathered for the reading of a will were shocked when the will began, "Being of sound mind, I spent every cent!"

A woman who believed that she could contact her dead husband sat down in the restaurant where he formerly worked, and said, "Gary? Gary, can you hear me?" "Yes, I can hear you," came his reply. "Gary!" she said. "It's so good to hear your voice. Can you come closer? I can barely hear you." "I can't come closer," he said. "That's not my table."

Happier Endings

If you've recently read a fairy tale to a child, then you know how hopelessly out of date they are. Today they're sexist, anti-democratic, and–what's worse–full of anti-step-parent propaganda. There's no excuse for repeating such stuff! If you've ever wished for more modern bed-time stories, your wish has just been granted. (Yes, fairy godmothers–I mean, fairy god persons–still exist.) When you again read aloud to the next generation, you can replace an over-the-hill fable with one of the following new and improved Happier Endings.

1. Cinderella met the prince, didn't like him, and eventually started her own house-cleaning service. Thanks to all her cleaning experience, she was a big success and retired young. Soon afterwards, she shacked up with an untitled–and brainless–hunk of beefcake, and lived happily ever after (periodically replacing the hunk).

2. The ugly duckling did NOT turn into a swan. Instead, he introduced the other ducks to sensitivity training, and they all learned not to taunt someone just because he was different from themselves. The duck saved up, sprang for major cosmetic surgery, and married a hot chick many years his junior.

3. Rudolph the Red-Nosed Reindeer sued the butcher who'd done the hatchet job on his schnozz and, with the proceeds from his case, bought a villa in Villefranche. He usually hangs out at a beach thronged with young American reindeer, where harnesses are optional.

4. One day a beautiful princess (actually, she had a

bumper crop of zits and some awesome "baby fat") happened to meet a frog. He told her, "If you bring me home and let me sleep in your bed, I will turn into a handsome prince." She took him to bed with her, and the next morning she found a handsome prince lying beside her. She couldn't believe what had happened, and neither could her parents.

5. Goldilocks was arrested for breaking and entering. She was also reprimanded by a conservation group for bothering endangered animals.

6. Dorothy was put on trial for killing the two witches. When the prosecutor heard that she had been involved with a whole field of poppies, he threw the book at her.

7. Snow White married a dwarf. She felt it was the right move because he was, after all, part owner of an extremely profitable diamond-and-gem mine. Later, this proved to be an even better move than she had thought, because all the inhabitants of the nearby castle were eventually beheaded by revolting peasants.

8. When the prince heard about the sleeping beauty in the tower, he said, "Do you honestly believe I would slash through 40 foot brambles just to wind up married? HELL, no!" He continued to troll the local singles' bars until he died of AIDS, and Sleeping Beauty slept on, eternally dreaming of a commitment. Which was just as well, because you know how crummy some women look after only ONE night. (How did the phrase "beauty sleep" originate, anyway?)

9. After Pinocchio had been brought to life, Gepetto spent hours kicking himself for the terrible mistake he'd

made. "I haven't had a woman in 20 YEARS," he moaned, "so why in the world did I wish for a lousy BOY?" Fortunately, he was able to talk the Good Fairy into making a trade. He lived in ecstasy ever after with a real living doll, whom he was careful not to deflate.

10. After Rumpelstiltskin challenged the princess to discover his name, she learned that he was involved with a Witness Relocation Program. Thanks to underworld connections, she was able to uncover his original identity, and when the mob found his hiding place, he was murdered in a ritual rubout.

12. When Little Red Riding Hood gave the Wolf a chance to explain, she found that things were not at all as she'd thought. He'd worn Grandma's dress because he was a transvestite and, as he said, "I simply ADORED her designer originals." Red, Granny and the Wolf were friends "forever after" talking fashion and doing mending.

13. The brick house of The Three Little Pigs was little more than a do-it-yourselfer, but it eventually sold for a cool half-mill due to its prime location. After it was bought by Japanese developers, the pigs encountered tragedy. The Wolf's relatives got their revenge–and the trio's remains were carried at small diners specializing in "homemade" pork chops.

14. The Pied Piper rid the town of Hamelin of all its mice and rats. When corrupt officials misappropriated the money he was owed, he sold the variously diseased rodents to several labs for big bucks.

Occupational Excuses

Every profession has its own arsenal of specialized excuses. Here are some dandies:

PLUMBER

After finishing a repair job on some pipes, a plumber announced, "That will be $200 for the last hour." "$200???," his customer said. "I'm a DOCTOR and I don't charge that much." "Neither did I, when I was a doctor," the plumber said.

Another plumber told a customer, "You owe me $201." "How is that possible?" the customer asked. "You've only been here for one minute and all you did was tap the pipe in a certain place. That can't be worth $201." "I charged $1 for the tap," the plumber explained, "and $200 for knowing where to tap."

Now is a good time to enter the lucrative field of plumbing. True, it's a dirty job–but somebody else might do it.

DOCTOR

A doctor wanted to join three colleagues for a late-night poker game, so he told his wife he had an emergency call. "How important is it?" she asked, and he said, "Let me put it this way, three doctors are already there!"

TELEVISION PRODUCER

A woman who returned from work earlier than usual

was stunned to find her husband (a television producer) in bed with another woman. Seeing her shock, he said, "Don't worry dear, she's just a summer replacement."

ELECTRICIAN

"Touch one of the two wires over there," an electrician told his assistant. His assistant did, and then asked why. Replied the electrician, "I knew one of the wires was 'live' but I didn't know which one."

HOUSEWIFE

One housewife dropped in to visit another on a day when the latter's children were driving her crazy. She told them, "Do whatever you want!" and her guest said, "Why don't you discipline them?" Explained her hostess, "This morning they disobeyed every rule I laid down–let's see them disobey THAT ONE!"

FLIGHT ATTENDANT

A flight attendant was working when a pilot announced, "THERE IS NO CAUSE FOR ALARM, BUT ONE OF OUR ENGINES HAS CONKED OUT. THIS SIMPLY MEANS THAT IT WILL TAKE US AN EXTRA HOUR TO REACH OUR DESTINATION." The flight attendant continued serving and, a while later, the pilot made the following announcement: "ANOTHER ENGINE HAS FAILED, BUT THERE IS STILL NO CAUSE FOR ALARM. IT WILL, HOWEVER, TAKE US *ANOTHER* HOUR TO REACH OUR DESTINATION." A short while later, the pilot made a third announcement: "...NO CAUSE FOR ALARM, BECAUSE WE STILL HAVE ONE ENGINE LEFT." The flight attendant said,

"This flight could get very boring. If that fourth engine goes, we'll be up here all night!"

BUSINESS TRIPS (FLYING)

One businessman said to another, "I have no fear of flying, but I am terribly afraid that my plane will be hijacked. I know the odds are a million-to-one that it will happen, but I can't help it." His friend said, "If you're so worried that someone will bring a bomb on board, then bring your OWN bomb. The odds will then be TWO-million-to-one that another passenger will have one."

DIVORCED TYCOON WEDS YOUNGER WOMAN

Just remember, many men owe their success to their first wife, and their second wife to their success.

PROFESSIONAL FUND-RAISER

A professional fund-raiser approached a millionaire and said, "Will you contribute money for the poor people in this town?" The millionaire said, "They don't deserve my charity. They just don't WANT to work." The fund-raiser said, "Look out the window. What do you see?" The millionaire said, "I just see...people." The fund-raiser said, "Now look in the mirror. What do you see?" The millionaire said, "I see myself." The fund-raiser said, "Isn't that amazing? When you're surrounded by silver, all you can see is yourself!"

PESSIMISTS (It may not be a profession, but they're certainly common!)

Two men were sitting opposite each other at an elegant banquet when one took an olive from the relish tray. He said, "Mmmmm," so the other man (who had never eaten an olive before) took one. He said, "Ugh!" and spat it out–while the first man took another and savored it. Seeing his enjoyment, the second man took another olive and, once again, said, "Ugh!" As he watched the first man enjoy a third olive, the second said, "He must be getting all the good ones."

I can't stand Jack Nicholson!" one friend told another. "How many of his movies have you seen?" his friend asked. "None!" he replied. "But I saw someone imitate him once, and he is TERRIBLE!"

TEACHER

When a student asked his teacher why she was failing him in history, she said, "Those who forget history are condemned to repeat it."

CHICKEN RANCHER

A poultry expert was asked, "Is it possible to develop a chicken with three drumsticks?" He said, "Not only is it possible–I've done it! Back on my ranch I have a huge flock of three-legged chickens." "What do they taste like?" he was asked. "I don't know, he said, no one can catch them!"

OPTIMISTS

There's only one really important thing to worry about in life–whether you're sick or well. If you're well, you have nothing to worry about. If you're sick, you only have one thing to worry about–whether you'll die or you'll recover. If you recover, you have nothing to worry about. If you die, you only have two things to worry about–if you'll go to heaven or hell. If you go to heaven, you'll have nothing to worry about. And if you go to hell, you'll be so busy greeting old friends that you won't have time to worry!

MATCHMAKER

A young man joined a matchmaking agency and viewed its videotapes. After he saw a young blonde's videotape, he said, "I'd like to meet her right away!" The matchmaker said, "Sorry, but you'll have to date an old lady first!" "Huh? Why?" the man said. The matchmaker replied, "Because this is a union shop–and those women have seniority!"

TEACHER

TEACHER TO STUDENT: Why was the Berlin Wall knocked down?
STUDENT: I didn't do it!
TEACHER TO SECOND TEACHER: I asked a student why the Berlin Wall was knocked down and he said he didn't do it.
SECOND TEACHER: The vandalism around here must be stopped!
TEACHER TO PRINCIPAL: I asked a student why the Berlin Wall was knocked down and, get this, he said he didn't do it.
PRINCIPAL: I'm really busy right now, but I'll see about getting it repaired as soon as possible!

MURDERER

WIDOW: My first husband ate some mushrooms and

died. My second husband also ate some mushrooms and died. I killed my third husband with a blunt instrument.
PROSECUTOR: Why did you do that?
WIDOW: Because he wouldn't eat the mushrooms.

DEBTOR (Is this an occupation? You tell me!)

I decided to pay off all my bills at once, because it's the only way I know to really get your money's worth.

CEO

UNDERLING: Hope this deal doesn't give you an ulcer.
BOSS: I don't get ulcers–I give 'em.

SOMEONE ON HIS OR HER FIRST JOB

CASHIER TO BAG BOY: Why are you so upset?
BAG BOY: I was told I'd get $4.50 an hour–but I've been working for three hours so far and I haven't gotten a penny yet!

EXPENSE ACCOUNT SPENDTHRIFTS

I spent most of the money on women and liquor–and the rest I spent foolishly!

PLAYBOY

One playboy's sister told him, "You ought to start saving some money. Don't spend it all on socializing. I go out on lots of dates and I save lots of money." Her brother said, "There's something you don't understand–what's making you rich is making me poor."

Good Deeds Will Not Go Without Punishment

Attempting to bring a little morality or some kindness into the world today can be a lot more difficult than it used to. Ask the "victims" in these significant stories...

A health education teacher told his class, "Think twice before you indulge in the pleasures of the flesh! One hour of earthly delight is not worth a lifetime of shame!" A student raised his hand after the teacher's statement and he thought, "At last I'm getting through to one of them!" The teacher said, "Do you have a question?" and the student said, "Yes. How do you make it last an hour?"

An underprivileged little boy wrote a letter to Santa Claus asking for $100. It came to the attention of a certain mailman. He and his fellow postal workers chipped in and managed to scrape up $70, which they sent to the little boy "from Santa." After Christmas, another letter arrived from the boy, and when they opened it, they read: "Dear Santa, thank you very much for the money you sent me. My family and I really appreciated receiving it. Next time, though, don't send it through the post office. The crooks there took out $30!"

A minister was passing a private house when he spotted a little boy straining to reach the doorbell. He went over and helped the little boy ring it, then said, "Would you like me to do anything else?" "Yeah!" said the little boy. "Run with me before they get to the door!"

A man rushed into a doctor's office and said, "Doctor, quick, tell me how to get rid of a bad case of hiccups?" The doctor immediately emptied a vase of water on him. "No, *I* don't have the hiccups!" he said. "It's my wife!"

A 7-year-old country boy was staring at an overturned wagon full of hay when a stranger came along and said, "What happened little boy?" "My father and I were driving along when our wagon turned over," he said. "Don't look so sad," the motherly woman said. "Why don't you come with me to this meadow and have some of the chicken I made?" "I don't think my father would like it," he said. "We're not far from the wagon. I'm sure he won't mind," the woman urged. The boy soon finished several pieces of chicken, and the woman said, "By the way, where is your father now?" "He's under the hay," answered the little boy.

A woman went to a very elegant, very expensive French restaurant. When she couldn't finish her meal, she asked for a doggy bag. "What's a 'doggy bag'?" asked the French waitress. "It's a bag of leftovers to feed my dog," the woman (who had no dog) answered. A few minutes later, the waitress brought her a bag and said, "I wanted your dog to have plenty, so I filled it with scraps from many different plates."

Excuses for Shrinks

Psychiatrists are people who get paid for "helping" others with lines such as, "What do YOU think?" and "My opinion doesn't matter." Anyone who goes to see a psychiatrist should have his head examined.

One psychiatrist said to another, "I can't stand it anymore! All day long I listen to people complaining, whining, moaning...How can you stand listening to them?" Said the second, "Who listens?"

A new patient told his psychiatrist, "I don't understand why my family told me to come see you. There's nothing wrong with me. I just like pancakes." The psychiatrist said, "I like pancakes, too." The patient said, "You DO? You must come to my house and see my collection. I've got trunks and trunks full of them!"

Three mothers were discussing the triumphs of their respective offspring. The first said, "My son is a doctor. He saved three lives last week!" The second said, "My son is an accountant. He saved a company thousands last month!" The third said, "My son sees a psychiatrist three times a week. And do you know what he talks about in every session? *ME*!"

Excuses to Offer Bullies

One well-muscled bruiser left his beer on the bar with a note next to it that read: I am the world's strongest man. This is my beer. I am coming right back." When he returned, the beer was gone, and there was a second note beside it that read: "I am the world's fastest man. I drank your beer, and I'm never coming back!"

A vacationing fullback taking in a football game was disturbed by a skinny guy, who said, "You're sitting in my seat." "Oh, yeah?" the player said, "How can you prove that it's your seat?" "I left my ice cream on it," the man answered.

A solidly-built woman ran for a cab that had been hailed by a man and climbed in triumphantly. The man handed several bills to the driver and said, "Drive around the block as long as this lasts!" The driver did so until the woman flounced out and the man jumped in!

A "98 pound weakling" who was taunted by punks as he walked home from school offered to pay them for bothering him. Every time they followed him home from school and called him names, he paid them each $1. After a while, he refused to pay them anymore and they refused to keep following him!

A man who attended the January white sale in a big department store was pushed and shoved from all sides by women stampeding for the bargains. At last he started doing some pushing and shoving of his own and a woman said, "Hey! Why don't you act like a gentleman?" He said, "I've been acting as a gentleman should for an hour and it's gotten me nowhere. Now I'm going to act like a lady!"

An arrogant woman told an eager suitor, "I wouldn't go out with you if you were the last man on earth!" He said, "You couldn't. You'd be trampled in the rush."

A woman found her son in bed one morning crying, "I don't want to go to school! The kids make fun of me, the teachers don't like me, and the principal thinks I'm an idiot!" She said, "You have to go. You're a teacher!"

A man went to a restaurant, tasted the chowder, and berated the waiter: "This is awful! I've tasted better!" The waiter said, "Not in this restaurant you haven't!"

Two hit men were waiting in an alley for their intended victim to walk by, but he didn't appear when they expected him to. At last one of them said, "Gosh, I hope nothing happened to him."

Now, Now, There's Really No Excuse for That!

There is NO excuse for the existence of many people, places and things in the world today. NONE, NONE, NONE! Unlike Gilbert and Sullivan, I don't have "a little list"–I have a BIIIIIIIIIG one! Here are just a few of the items on it:

1. Star Trek coventions

The whole phenomenon has gotten way out of hand. Did you know that people have gotten MARRIED wearing Spock ears and Star Fleet uniforms? Did you know there are people (perhaps that's the wrong word) who CARE what the "T" in "James T. Kirk stands for? Did you know there are a slew of magazines in which Kirk and Spock–shall we say–go steady? SHEESH!

2. People who don't want animals used in experiments to save human lives.

They mostly use RATS for such experiments–and, in case you never noticed, VERY FEW people have ever made coats from these animals!

3. Commercials in which the toilet paper talks.

Last time I reached for a package of the stuff, I swear I heard it plead, "You *WOULDN'T*!" And I didn't have the heart, so I bought another brand...advertisers, take note!

4. Long traffic lights when you're driving.

5. Short traffic lights when you're walking.

6. People who keep big dogs in small apartments.

7. Horse carriages on the streets on Manhattan.

I suspect Manhattan has a lot of inbred backwoodsmen who cram their studio apartments with Great Danes and Dobermans, drive carriages for a living, and are working on a plan to bring their good buddy, Marvin the Moose, to midtown.

8. Cigarette commercials that depict (HACK!) happy, (CHOKE!) healthy (GASP!) people bursting with life (COUGH! COUGH!).

9. Television shows that depict a lot of drinking but rarely mention hangovers, drunk driving, or alcoholism.

10. Television shows that depict a lot of fooling around but never mention birth control, venereal disease, AIDS or love.

11. Parties featuring big buffet platters that are hardly touched before they're discarded.

12. The computer-corrected tests given in schools that read, "PRESS HARD or the computer won't record your answers. And BE SURE to ERASE every SLIGHT, stray pencil mark or the computer will POSITIVELY PICK IT UP." Why don't they make up their minds?

13. Kids who say, "I can't tell the time from that clock–I can only read digital ones."

14. Students who rent the movie instead of reading the assigned book.

15. The incredible boring way in which some grade school textbooks are written.

16. Lottery ticket buyers who think they have a good chance of winning big, particularly if they crack open their nest eggs to buy some. The yolk's on them!

17. People who say, "I refuse to take pennies."

18. The fact that Halloween has become a day on which a number of people become ghosts–permanently.

19. People who treat street lights with open bases as though they were trash bins. And that goes double for people who use clothing collection boxes for garbage.

20. Call waiting.

21. Newscasters who turn personal human tragedies into clips for "Film at 11."

22. Movies that feature graphic, exotic murders but no lines about the value of every human life.

23. If you are pressured to take drugs, here's one excuse you can use: "Take drugs? Why bother? I already spend one-third of my life dead to the world!"

Or you could say, "Losing your head can lead to losing lots of other things. I knew a guy who smoked so much pot that he had to go to Arizona for his lungs!"

Be like ace writer Harlan Ellison–he's "high on life!"

An Ode to Classic Excuses

Can't take that route, it's much too far.

Won't take the bus, don't have a car.

Can't pass this test, this course is too hard.

Don't have the cash, no credit card.

Can't contact you, not near a phone.

Must bring a friend, can't go alone.

My car won't start, just missed the trains.

Will not make up, don't need the pain.

Someone just misplaced your fax.

There was a fire on the tracks.

Those two...like monkeys in a cage!

Can't act like that, not at my age.

It looks like rain, don't have time.

You need a witness to the crime.

My horoscope says, "No can do."

And that's the word from my guru.

We've lived before, and were close then, so let us get that close again.

My daughter's ill, the rent is due.

Do what you said, or else I'll sue.

There was too much traffic on the way.

A tie-up causes a big delay.

I never did that thing before.

I'll never do it anymore.

I sent the check on Monday last, but postal clerks are never fast.

My subway car on tracks did stall.

My car was stolen at the mall.

It is too hot, it is too cold.

Can't call a man, that is too bold.

I never wear much makeup, I was born this way, and that's no lie.

This flab was passed to me by Ma; it wouldn't help to pay a spa.

I saw that film just for research; I'm with a special group from church.

The airline bumped me from my seat.

I've really had too much to eat.

Sorry I can't stay too long.

Oh, our computer's never wrong.

I took it back because I have two; I cherish every gift from you.

Twist and Shout

Life is full of twists and turns–twisted logic, turns of fortune and licorice twists. Read on for some more.

A student who was meeting with his professor was very surprised to see a large horseshoe hanging over the professor's door. He said, "How can a brilliant, learned man as yourself believe in such a silly superstition?" "Oh, I don't believe in it at all," the professor answered. "But I've heard that even if you don't believe in it, it brings you luck."

A man who had been hired to empty the coins from parking meters disappeared on payday. When he resurfaced the following Monday, his boss asked him, "Why didn't you pick up the money that you earned last week?" The man smiled broadly and said, "You mean I get *PAID, TOO*?"

A patron in a small coffee shop said, "I want to order some burned toast, cold coffee and stale orange juice." The waitress said, "I can't serve you those things," and he said, "Why not? You did yesterday."

A customer at an elegant restaurant angrily summoned his waiter and said, "Taste this soup!" "I'm sure there's nothing wrong with it," the waiter said, "it's the chef's specialty." "TASTE IT!" the man demanded. "I had it for lunch and I loved it," the waiter said. "TASTE IT!" the man insisted. "I can replace it if you'd like me to," the waiter said, but the diner just repeated, "TASTE IT!" Finally, the waiter decided to taste the soup, and reached for the man's spoon. "You didn't get a spoon," he blurted out, and the diner triumphantly said, "*AHA*!"

One mother asked her younger daughter, "Why don't you get married, like your sister Sharon did? Sharon's life is the perfect life for a woman," she went on, "Sharon has a husband and five children, a nice home AND a part-time job!"

Her younger daughter protested, "But Mom, every day Sharon comes home from work and starts taking care of her children and husband. After she finishes the cooking, the cleaning, and all the other chores, she rarely has time for herself–and she never has any money.

"I, on the other hand, HAVE a great life. My time time and my money are entirely my own. I own a luxurious apartment, a Mercedes, and a mink coat, also, I'm going to Acapulco this winter. I can come and go as I please, do whatever I want, and I look 10 years younger than Sharon did at my age."

"You're right," her mother admitted, "your life is much better than hers, but could you do one special favor for me?" "What's that?" her younger daughter asked. "Don't tell Sharon!" her mother said.

A man walking through a golf course was accidentally bopped with a ball. When he pulled himself together, he told the golfer at fault, "I'm going to sue you! I'm going to sue you for $10,000!" "Didn't you hear me yell, 'Fore'?" the golfer said. "No, but I'll take it," the bruised and bleeding man replied.

Two men waiting in a doctor's office were talking about the doctor's terrible handwriting. "Isn't it awful?" the first one said. "I'm always afraid that the pharmacist will misread one of his prescriptions and give me something fatal!" The other said, "I think it's wonderful that he writes so illegibly. Last time he gave me a prescription, my daughter played it on the piano and my son used it to get into Yankee Stadium!"

A teacher was encouraging her students to buy their school's yearbook. "In years to come," she said, "you will look at the pictures and say things such as, 'There's Bruce, he's a writer' and 'There's Emma, she's an artist'." One student added, "And we'll say, 'There's Teacher, she's dead'!"

One depressed man invited a co-worker to his home for dinner. The moment he got home, he took off his shoes and said, "Ahhhhh! Does that feel good!" His friend said, "You shouldn't wear such tight shoes. Why don't you get a bigger size so your feet won't hurt all day?" "Let me tell you something," the other man replied. "I HATE my job. Every day the boss yells at me, the customers give me grief and the commuting drives me crazy. Every day I need something to look forward to, at the end of the day–and taking off my tight shoes is always a JOY!"

A man went to a psychiatrist and said, "I'm here because I turned into a dog." The psychiatrist said, "Lie down." The man said, "I can't. I'm not allowed to sit on the couch."

A man was leafing through some classified ads when he spotted one he just couldn't believe. It read, "1989 Mercedes for Sale. Perfect condition, only $10." He knew that there must be some catch, but he hurried over to the address in the ad and asked to see it anyway. When he found that it was perfect, he immediately wrote out a check for $10. As he handed it to the woman who had placed the ad, he asked, "Why are you selling it so cheaply?" She said, "My husband died recently. In his will, he instructed me to sell his Mercedes and give the money to his secretary."

A boss noticed that one of his employees, a file clerk, drove a fancy car–lived in a fancy apartment–and ate in fancy restaurants. He couldn't figure out how he could afford all that on his salary, and finally asked him how he did it. The clerk explained, "Each week I raffle off my salary. Last week I sold a thousand chances at $2 each."

In Search of Excuses

There are certain things for which no excuse can be found (at least, not by me). But, hey, life is a journey, not a destination, so there are many questions without answers, such as these:

WHAT EXACTLY DISTINGUISHES "FUN FOODS" FROM OTHER FOODS?

If some foods are "fun foods," are other foods "serious foods" or "unfun foods?" (If there are "junk foods," shouldn't there be "valuable foods?" Just wondering.)

I assume that "fun foods" are a separate food group inadvertently left off nutrition charts because so many supermarket items are labeled that way.

There ARE many clues about the mysterious category of "fun foods." They always come in bizarre colors and strange shapes. They are foods not found in nature (and seemingly not on this planet) but not all "unnatural" foods are "fun." (I think eating granola is unnatural.)

They're often described as foods eaten by various imaginary creatures such as super heroes, leprechauns, talking animals and kids that are in ecstasy when they eat bizarrely-colored, strangely-shaped foods.

I've noticed that people in real life rarely experience the "rush" felt by people in commercials when both groups eat the same "fun food." It must be a matter of differing chemical compositions, perhaps involving mutated metabolisms. The fact is (REALLY, THIS IS TRUE) some people naturally form LSD in their bloodstreams.

It has been my experience that the foods kids find most enjoyable are the foods they get to throw. Peak enjoyment is experienced when the food is thrown in the school cafeteria, and a bullseye is scored on a particularly unpopular kid.

But I digress. I theorize that certain bizarre colors and strange shapes are "more fun" than certain other bizarre colors and strange shapes. If this is the case, then things are far more complicated than I thought. Could it be (this is just a theory, mind you) that food is "the most fun of all" when its mix of colors and shapes evokes the average "Clash Day" outfit?

Why the focus on color and shapes, anyway? There are other senses. Why is there only one cereal (that I know of) that "talks?" People apparently never tire of hearing its meaningless mantra, "Snap, crackle, pop" but I, for one, seek a deeper meaning. Since many dolls sold today talk more than the average stool pigeon, why can't cereals do the same? If snap, crackle, pop wows 'em, consider what something really significant would do. The possibilities are infinite. Technology that can produce a Pee-Wee Herman doll that says, "I know you are, but what am I?" can no doubt create a cereal that says, "I think, therefore I am." I can visualize a perfect ad campaign for one such high-tech breakfast food: "CLIFFHANGER CEREAL. IT TELLS A NEW STORY EVERY WEEK."

IN MOST FAIRY TALES, WHY ARE THE GOOD CHARACTERS ALWAYS BEAUTIFUL, AND THE BAD CHARACTERS ALWAYS UGLY?

All good people ARE beautiful, of course, when they're judged by their deeds, and the reverse is also true. It's too bad that this fact is usually not apparent to children in today's world, a world in which a certain popular doll, if she were alive, would have anorexia.

IF YOU CAN GET AN "OFFICIAL" SEX CHANGE AND AN "OFFICIAL" RELIGION CHANGE, WHY AREN'T MORE IMPORTANT CHANGES PERMITTED?

Wouldn't you like an age change? Maybe your mandatory retirement age is coming up and you don't want to retire. You could have your age officially changed from, say, 60 to 50. Or 40. Or 30. Twice a year we're forced to accept the idea that time has moved forward or back by one hour, so why shouldn't people accept age changing? How about "official" background changing? Everyone could then become Irish on St. Patrick's Day for real. How about one big era change for everybody? Most of us miss the 50s, so why don't we have the 90s officially changed to that time? Can I see a show of hands?

Real Life Excuses

I heard these excuses with my own ears. Truth is stranger than fiction, but it's usually not as entertaining.

A certain store contains a department in which there are three doors in a row. One is labeled "MEN," one is labeled "WOMEN" and one is labeled "CLOSET." A little boy parked himself in front of these doors and refused to move when his mother urged him along. She said, "Why don't you come with me?" and he said, "Because I heard on TV that more men these days are coming out of the closet, and I wanted to see if that's true!"

A man watching an ultrasound "movie" of his unborn child looked bored, and his wife said, "What's the matter? Isn't this fascinating?" He said, "I couldn't be more interested, but I was wondering what programs are on the other channels."

A student's assignment was to go to the library and get an example of "prose poetry." She picked a book of poetry by one author, went to the librarian and asked, "He's a pro, isn't he?"

A student in a special education class lacked a wide variety of basic skills. Whenever a teacher pointed out one of his mistakes, the student refused to cooperate with him/her. In a conversation with a classmate, he said smugly, "They tell me what I can't do, but I tell them what I ain't gonna do!"

I heard a woman in a pizza store say, "Things are really different in the world today." The man to whom she said this didn't understand English very well, and asked her to repeat it. After she had repeated it, he still looked confused, and she said, "The world. THE WORLD! You know–New York!"

A man in a photo shop asked the woman behind the counter to restore an old photograph. He said, "I want you to take the hat off of this man's head." She asked, "Which way did he part his hair?" and he said, "You'll find out when you take his hat off."

Overheard: "Oh, the Halloween Parade is an actual parade in Greenwich Village? I thought it referred to what's always in the streets there."

One excuse you should never use in New York is, "I'm late because I was delayed by the Easter Parade." The Easter Parade is not an actual parade, but an expression referring to the people who dress up on Easter and parade in the street (particularly people who parade down Fifth Avenue after St. Patrick's Cathedral services let out.) This enlightening fact is an added bonus for buying this book!

And Still Yet Another Assortment of Excuses

A man who had bet on a slow horse was amazed to see him go from last place to first–after the jockey whispered in his ear. At the end of the race, he asked the jockey, "What did you tell him?" The jockey replied, "I just recited a little poem: 'Roses are red/Violets are blue/Horses that lose/are made into glue'."

A man heard about the wonderful apple pie in a certain restaurant and decided to go there. He took a cab to a train to a bus to a boat to a jeep to a plane to a cable car, walked in and ordered apple pie. The waitress said, "We're fresh out." He said, "OK, I'll take blueberry."

Another man (maybe it was the same one, come to think of it) took a cab to a train to a plane to a jeep to an elephant to a boat to another boat...(well, you get the picture)...to a car to a trolley...and arrived at a friend's house. He rang the doorbell, and when his friend answered, he said, "I just happened to be in the neighborhood, so I thought I'd drop by."

A man who had spent years training a dog to perform in the movies was using him to impress a girl. He told her, "He's so smart that when I attach money to his collar, he'll take it to the candy store and get us some chocolate bars." The dog went out and didn't return for hours. When he finally came back, he had a female dog with him. The trainer turned to the girl and said, "You have to understand–I never gave him money before."

A 10-year-old boy once left this note for his mother: "Jeffrey and I will be out skateboarding until 10 p.m. Is that all right with you?"

A little boy was just at the age when kids love to say "No!" As he went around the house saying it over and over, his mother said, "I'm sure he'll have a photographic memory when he grows up." Her friend asked why, and she said, "Because his mind is so full of negatives."

A famous artist was passing through a rural area when he saw an old man that he thought would be a perfect subject for his next painting. He went up to him and asked, "Would you take $100 in exchange for letting me paint you?" The old man hesitated, and the artist said, "Why are you reluctant? Do you want more money?" The old man said, "It's not that. I was just wondering how I would get the paint off afterwards."

A famous violin player still practiced five hours a day at the age of 90. When a reporter asked him why he did this, he said, "I think I'm beginning to get it right."

A couple brought their baby to be baptized and the wife said, "We're naming this one Jack; just Jack. Don't put down anything else." The minister said, "Why would I do that?" She said, "Last year when we were getting our last son baptized, we told you we were naming him Tom–but you wrote down THOMAS."

One teacher told her class, "There are two words I never want you to use. One is GRODY and the other is RAD." A student asked, "What are the words?"

A little boy was taken to visit Santa Claus in a department store by his mother, and he told Santa exactly what he wanted for Christmas. When he went to visit his father, he was taken to another department store Santa. That Santa said, "Ho-ho-ho, little boy, what can I do for you?" The little boy kicked him and said, "Don't you remember what I told you?"

One 10-year-old said to another, "Look! There's 50 cents on the sidewalk." The second said, "That must be the 50 cents I lost here before." The second said, "It can't be. You lost a half dollar and there are two quarters here." The first said, "It's MY 50 cents. The half dollar must have broken when it hit the sidewalk."

On another occasion, some kid was looking all around a side street for some change he had lost. His friend came along and asked him, "You lost your money on Main Street, didn't you? Why don't you look over there?" The kid said, "The light's better over here."

The following story is dedicated to all performers everywhere, particularly Trevor Hasselfree's troupe:

A man suffering from severe depression went to a psychiatrist and said, "I don't know HOW to relieve my depression, doctor. Can you help me?" The doctor said, "I have the perfect cure for you. One of the world's greatest clowns has just arrived here with a traveling circus. Go to see him and I guarantee that he'll cheer you up." "There's something you don't understand," the man said. " I AM that clown."

One woman said to another, "I'm not married because I can't decide between Bob and Bruce. I wish their good points could be combined into one man." Her friend asked, "What are their good points?" and the woman said, "Bob is rich, handsome, charming and intelligent. And Bruce wants to marry me!"

"Why are you in such a bad mood this morning?" one co-worker asked another. "Did you wake up grumpy?" "No, he got up before I did," she answered.

Two women who hadn't seen each other since their college graduation were comparing notes on their lives. The first said, "I married a millionaire, and we live in a fabulous mansion with indoor and outdoor swimming pools." "Fantastic!" the other woman said. "We have a Jaguar and a Mercedes," she went on, "and 12 servants." The other woman repeated, "Fantastic!" "Next week we're going on a trip around the world," the second added. Once again, the other woman said, "Fantastic!" "How about you?" the first woman asked. "What have you been doing?" "I married a file clerk," she said. "We don't have much money, and we don't have a very nice apartment, but I recently went to 'finishing school'." "Really!" her friend said. "Whatever did you learn while you were there?" "I learned to say, 'Fantastic!' instead of 'Bull'!" she said.

A man looking out the window of his apartment said to his wife, "Look–there goes the woman that my friend Alan is terribly in love with." His wife rushed to the window and said, "That's his wife!" "Of course," replied her husband.

A boy who had almost drowned in a lake was being treated by paramedics, and one said, "Give him artificial respiration." His father, hovering nearby, said, "Give him the real thing! I can afford it!"

A man was being given an Army medical exam, and the doctor asked, "When was the last time you had sex?" He said, "1959." The doctor said, "1959??" The patient said, "What's wrong with that? It's only 2230 now!"

The hostess of a party asked a guest if he was enjoying himself. He said, "Yes, I'm enjoying myself, but he sounded bored. The hostess asked, "Are you sure you're enjoying yourself?" and the guest said, "Yes, I AM enjoying myself–but that's all I'm enjoying!"

When a visitor at a party heard that one of the guests was an ex-minister, he asked him, "Were you defrocked or just unsuited?"

A bar owner was awakened at 3 a.m. by a telephone call. The man on the line asked, "What time does your bar open?" The bar owner said, "Not for hours!" and hung up. The man called back and asked the same question, and, once again, the bar owner hung up on him. The phone rang a third time, and the bar owner shouted into the receiver, "You can't get into the bar until noon!" The man on the phone protested, "I don't want to get in! I want to get out!"

One woman attending a performance of *Hamlet* turned to another and said, "I don't know why they say this play is so great. It's nothing but a bunch of familiar quotations strung together!"

A man rushed into a police station and said, "I was mugged! Two men surprised me, hit me and took all the money I had!" A cop said, "That's terrible! When did this happen?" He said, "Fifteen years ago–but I like to get some more sympathy once in a while."

A man performing before a reserved British audience was surprised when no one laughed at his act. He tried as hard as he could to amuse them, but they sat silently and didn't even smile. Afterwards, a woman came backstage and said, "Your act was hysterical! It was so funny that we could hardly keep from laughing."

All right, it's not true that British people are reserved–but it is hard to book one at the last minute.

A man was waiting for his date in a fancy restaurant when he spotted his favorite actor, Richard Dreyfuss, eating there. He went over to him and said, I've seen all of your pictures and I think you're wonderful. Would you do me a big favor? When my date comes in, could you greet me as though we were old friends?" The actor said he would. A short while later, he went over to the couple's table and said, "Hi there. How are you doing? I haven't seen you in a long time!" The man scowled at him and said, "How many times have I asked you not to bother me while I'm eating?"

During his psychiatry session, a patient said, "...and another thing, doctor, I often talk to myself." The psychiatrist said, "There's nothing wrong with that. A lot of people talk to themselves." The patient said, "I know...but I'm SO BORING!"

While driving around with his date, a young man took one hand off the wheel and reached our for her. "Use both hands!" she snapped. "I can't," he said. "I have to drive with one!"

A man who had just had a medical exam said, "Don't give me a lot of medical double-talk, doctor. Tell me, in plain language, what's wrong with me." His doctor said, "To tell the truth, you're lazy." The man said, "Now give me a medical term that I can give my wife."

A young man spoke to a financial advisor on a radio show and asked, "Is is possible to live 'the good life' on $200 a week?" The advisor said, "When you only make $200, 'being good' is all you can afford to do!"

A woman who was dying told her husband, "When I'm dead, give my dresses to your second wife." He said, "I could never do that." She said, "I insist, I want you to do that." He said, "I couldn't, it's impossible." She said, "Why not?" and he said, "Because she's a size 8 and you're a size 12."

A man went to a marriage counselor and said, "My marriage has really gotten monotonous. What can I do to put some new excitement into it?" The counselor said, "Why don't you try making love in a brand new place? The next time you have dinner with your wife, make your move on the dining room table!" During the man's next visit a week later, the counselor said, "Did you follow my suggestion?" "I certainly did!" the man said. "It worked wonderfully! My wife and I scattered the silverware and went wild! There's one problem, though." "What's that?" the counselor asked. "They're NEVER letting us in that restaurant AGAIN!" he said.

A woman walked into a boutique and said, "That sign in your window is misspelled. It should say 'b-a-r-g-a-i-n-s' not 'b-a-r-g-e-n-s'." The boutique owner said, "I know that. But most of the people who come in to tell me about the sign end up buying something!"

One boss breaking in a new employee said, "When a salesman calls, don't say 'yes' to ANYTHING he says; they can be very tricky." A salesman called and the boss listened in as his new employee spoke. "No...no...no...yes...no...no...no." After he hung up, his boss said, "What was that 'yes' for?" "He asked me if I could hear him," his employee explained.

An executive hired an attractive but dumb secretary, and asked him to look up the number of Zoltan Zinc. Fifteen minutes later, she asked him if he had gotten the number yet, and he said, "I'm up to 'G' now."

A teacher questioned a student in class and heard no response, so he asked, "Do you know the answer?" "Of course I do," the student replied. "Didn't you see me shake my head?" The teacher said, "You didn't think I could hear it rattle way up here, did you?"

Yet another man who visited his doctor for a medical exam was told to stick his tongue out the window. "Why should I do that?" he asked. "Because I'm mad at my neighbor," the doctor replied.

A man went to court to have his name changed, and the judge asked him what his name was. "It's Joe Stinkowitz," he said, "I understand why you're changing it," said the judge. "What are you changing it to?" "Jack Stinkowitz," the man said. "Why on earth are you changing it to that?" the judge asked. "Because I'm tired of hearing my friends say, 'Hello, Joe, what do you know'?" the man explained.

This story is for ASPCA director Kathy Travers. A woman who had just picked up her child from a day-care center said, "I never heard such an insult in my life! Another child's mother said my child looks like a monkey!" Another mother beside her said, "How terrible! I hope this cookie will make you feel better. And here's a banana for your monkey."

A couple who had made plans to see a Billy Joel concert decided to five the ticket money to a poor couple instead. As soon as the poor couple got the money, they rushed out and bought tickets to the Billy Joel concert!

A man was dying and he said, "When I die, will you put $1,000 in my coffin?" His friend said, "Sure I will." A few days later, one of the man's survivors asked his friend, "Did you put that money in the coffin?" He asked, "I certainly did. Here's the check stub."

A mother was quizzing her little boy about honesty and asked, "If you found $50,000 in the street, would you return it to the owner?" "If a poor person had lost it, I would," he said.

A man who was collecting for a charity approached a rich man and was promptly told to leave. "I asked your son for a donation, and *he* gave one to me," the man said. The millionaire bellowed, "*He* has a rich father, but unfortunately I don't!"

A business executive was extremely annoyed when she learned that her flight had been overbooked. She was very anxious to get on the plane, so she said, "If President Bush showed up, you would get him a seat, wouldn't you?" The clerk said, "Yes, we would." She said, "He's not coming, so give me his seat!"

A nurse picked up a phone in a hospital and a voice said, "How is the patient in Room 307?" The nurse consulted a chart and said, "The patient in Room 307 is doing fine. In fact, he'll probably be discharged in a couple of days. Who is this?" The caller said, "I'm the patient in Room 307–but my doctor didn't tell me anything!"

When a man noticed a certain best-seller on a friend's shelf, he asked if he could borrow it. "You can read it," his friend said, "but only in my house. I don't want my books to leave my sight." A while later, the man who owned the book asked to borrow his friend's lawnmower. "You can borrow it as long as it doesn't leave my lawn," his friend replied.

A woman who hadn't seen a certain friend in quite a while was amazed to run into her–and her new triplets. "Triplets! Isn't that something!" she said. "Yes, it certainly is," the proud mother replied. "The doctor told me that it only happens once in 10,000 times." "My goodness," her friend exclaimed, "when do you find time to do the housework?"

A man on his vacation spotted a wrinkled, gray-haired man by the pool who was smoking and drinking in the company of many women. He went over to him and said, "I must congratulate you, sir. You obviously believe in living life to the fullest and you have more stamina than any man your age. Would you mind telling me just how old you are?" The "old" man said, "I don't mind at all. I'm 19."

A man met another in a bar who said, "My name is Joe and I think I'm the most popular man in the world." The other man said, "That's ridiculous. Prove it." Joe turned to the people in the bar and said, "Who am I?" and a chorus of voices responded, "You're my good buddy, Joe! My old friend, my best pal" and so on. The other man said, "All right, you have good friends in this bar. But let's go somewhere else." They went to another bar and a similar scene was repeated. The man said, "All right, you have friends in two bars. What about the rest of the world?" Joe said, "Come with me." They got into a cab, and the cab driver said, "Joe! It's so great to see you again! Where can I take you–for free, of course?" Joe said, "Take us to the airport." When they got to the airport, Joe was greeted by the ticket sellers and they promptly boarded a plane to Washington–without paying, of course. On board, all the passengers, the flight attendants and the pilot greeted Joe, and when they got off, everyone in the airport waved to him. They soon arrived at the White House and Joe told his new friend, "Wait here." In a moment, President Bush emerged from the house, chatting happily with Joe. A man standing next to the stunned bar patron said, "Who's that over there?" The patron raised an eyebrow and said, "Oh, don't you know Joe?" The man said, "Of course I know Joe. But who's the man with him?"

A little girl saw her father preparing a sermon and she asked, "Does God tell you what to write?" "Yes, He does," her father answered. "Then why do you keep crossing things out?" she asked.

A man in a bar said, "That looks like the pope sitting over there at the bar! I just have to go over to him and find out if he is." He went up to the man and said, "Pardon me, but are you the pope?" The man said, "You disgusting drunk! Get away from me or I'll punch your lights out!" The man turned away sadly and said, "Now

I'll never know."

A woman told her husband, "Whenever I'm down in the dumps, I get a new blouse." He said, "Oh. I've been wondering where you get them."

One agitated broker asked another, "How did you sleep last night!" "Like a baby!" he replied. "Really?" the other asked. "Absolutely!" he said. "I cried and wet the bed all night!"

Before the days of OTB, bookies handled all off-track betting. A minister once noticed a man on the street to whom many people gave envelopes of money. He put money in an envelope, wrote "Bless You" on it and gave it to the man. A few days later, the man came to him and said, "Here are your winnings. 'Bless You' won the race, at 10-to-1 odds!"